David's Wings: The Strategic Development Of The Israeli Air Force

By Lt. Col. Kelly-KGB-Borukhovich

Contents

Publishing Information — ii
    Bibliographic Key Phrases ii
    Publisher's Note ii
    Truth in Publishing: Disclosures iii
    Analytic Table of Contents v

Abstracts — viii
    ELI5 viii
    Scientific-Style Abstract viii
    Mnemonics ix

Most Important Passages — x

Glossary for Modern Readers — xii
    Glossary for Lay Readers xvi

Index of Persons — xxiii

Index of Places — xxv

Innovative Indexes based on "David's Wings: The Strategic Development of the Israeli Air Force" — xxix
    Index 1: Evolutionary Factors and Inflection Points xxix
    Index 2: Major Operations and Campaigns xxix
    Index 3: Key Themes and Concepts xxx

Timeline — xxxii

Publishing Information

Nimble Books LLC: The AI Lab for Book-Lovers

~ Fred Zimmerman, Editor ~

Humans and AI making books richer, more diverse, and more surprising.

(c) 2024 Nimble Books LLC - ISBN: 978-1-60888-322-6

Bibliographic Key Phrases

Israeli Air Force; IAF Evolution; National Strategy; Air Power; Strategic Tool; Small State Air Force; Existential Threat; Inflection Points; Operation Moked; Operation Thunderbolt; Operation Babylon; Operation Wooden Leg; Yom Kippur War; War of Attrition; Six Day War; Arab-Israeli Wars; Israeli Defense Forces; IDF; Suez Canal Crisis; Counterterrorism; Preemptive Strike; Nuclear Deterrence; Strategic Attack; Strategic Effect; Air-mindedness; Technology Acquisition; UAVs; Helicopters; Command and Control; Electronic Warfare; Quality and Standards; Joint Operations; Multirole Aircraft; Combined Arms;

Publisher's Note

The Middle East is a volatile and dangerous region, and the Israeli Air Force (IAF) has played a crucial role in ensuring the security of the Jewish state since its inception in 1947. This thesis delves into the fascinating evolution of the IAF, exploring its transformation from a tactical force focused on defending Israel's borders to a strategic tool of national power capable of striking targets thousands of miles away.

Lieutenant Colonel Kelly "KGB" Borukhovich traces the IAF's development, highlighting key inflection points and factors that shaped its growth. The document meticulously analyzes pivotal operations, including the Six Day War, the Yom Kippur War, Operation Thunderbolt (Entebbe), Operation Babylon (Osirak), and Operation Wooden Leg, showcasing the IAF's adaptability, technological prowess, and tactical brilliance.

This thesis is a must-read for anyone seeking to understand the intricate dynamics of air power in a complex geopolitical environment. Whether you are a researcher, practitioner, policymaker, or simply someone interested in the Middle East, this document provides invaluable insights into the IAF's operational history, its impact on Israeli national security, and its enduring influence on the global stage. You will gain a deeper understanding of the factors that have shaped the IAF's evolution and the challenges it continues to face in the 21st century.

Truth in Publishing: Disclosures

Context: DAVID'S WINGS: THE STRATEGIC DEVELOPMENT OF THE ISRAELI AIR FORCE, a thesis presented to the School of Advanced Air and Space Studies (SAASS) at Air University by Lt Col Kelly "KGB" Borukhovich in June 2019.

Strengths:

- **A Deep Dive into Israeli Air Power:** This thesis offers a detailed look at the evolution of the Israeli Air Force (IAF), focusing on its strategic development rather than just operational narratives.
- **Comprehensive Timeline:** The work covers a significant period from the IAF's inception in 1947 to 1985, encompassing key conflicts and turning points.
- **Inflection Points:** Borukhovich does a good job highlighting the impact of key figures like Dan Tolkovski and Benny Peled on the IAF's evolution, demonstrating their influence on doctrine and acquisition.
- **Recognizes the Unique Context:** The thesis acknowledges the IAF's unique origins and operates within the challenging context of Israel's geopolitical environment.

Weaknesses:

- **The "David and Goliath" Trope:** The thesis leans heavily on the "David and Goliath" metaphor, which, while understandable given Israel's circumstances, can feel a bit cliché and overused.

- **Repetitive Language:** Some phrases like "near-constant existential threat" are repeated frequently, making the text a bit repetitive.
- **A Touch of "Air Force Speak":** The writing can be a bit dense, peppered with military jargon that might deter casual readers.

- **Lack of Critical Analysis:** While the thesis provides a solid historical overview, it could benefit from a more critical analysis of the IAF's successes and failures, especially in the context of its strategic objectives.

- **Bias:** Like most works on the Israeli-Arab conflict, the thesis tends to reflect an Israeli perspective.

Overall:

This is a well-researched and informative piece, but it could benefit from a more nuanced and less formulaic approach to the subject matter. Readers interested in a straightforward account of the IAF's development will find this thesis a useful resource, but those seeking a more critical or multi-faceted analysis might be left wanting more.

Disclaimer: This "Truth in Publishing" abstract is intended to be light-hearted and humorous, but the author is ultimately responsible for the content of their thesis.

Analytic Table of Contents

Introduction: A David in a World of Goliaths

- The unique geopolitical context of Israel's founding and its constant struggle for survival.
- The challenges of building a modern air force in a state under immediate threat.
- The IAF's transition from a purely reactive force to a strategic instrument of national power.
- The central question: What factors have influenced the evolution of the IAF from 1947 to the present?

Chapter 1: Birth in Fire: The IAF in the War for Independence (1948-1949)

- The Sherut Avir: Israel's fledgling air service before independence.
- The limitations of the IAF's initial inventory: civilian aircraft and improvised weaponry.
- The IAF's early roles: reconnaissance, transport, and rudimentary bombing.
- The evolving role of air power in the War of Independence: from ground support to air-to-air combat.
- Operation Yoav: The IAF's first major offensive operation and its impact on the war.

Chapter 2: The Long Shadow of Victory: The IAF from 1950 to the Eve of the Six-Day War

- The impact of the War of Independence on IAF development: personnel loss and limited budgets.
- The arrival of Major General Dan Tolkovski: a visionary leader who reshaped the IAF.
- Tolkovski's philosophy: quality over quantity, multirole aircraft, and continuous rigorous training.
- The acquisition of jet fighters: The IAF enters the jet age.
- The Suez Canal Crisis: A proving ground for the IAF's new doctrine and capabilities.
- Lessons learned: The need for strategic reserves, air superiority, and rapid deployment.

Chapter 3: The Price of Success: The IAF in the Six-Day War and the War of Attrition

- The Six-Day War: The IAF's triumph in Operation Moked and the attainment of air superiority.
- The impact of the Six-Day War on the international balance of power: Increased Soviet and US involvement.

- The War of Attrition: A brutal, protracted conflict that tested the IAF's resilience and adaptability.
- The evolution of the IAF's mission set: From CAS and air superiority to deep strikes and suppression of enemy air defenses.
- The role of the Soviet Union: The introduction of advanced SAM systems and the growing threat to IAF operations.
- Operation Priha: A turning point in the War of Attrition.
- The IAF's reliance on new US technology: The F-4 Phantom and the Skyhawk.
- Yom Kippur War: The unexpected Arab offensive and the IAF's initial struggles.
- The importance of intelligence: The need for timely and accurate information to guide operations.
- The IAF's use of deception and survival techniques to overcome the threat of advanced SAM systems.
- The significance of the air raid on the Syrian General Command: A strategic strike with both retaliatory and deterrent objectives.

Chapter 4: The Long Arm of David: The IAF in the Post-Yom Kippur Era

- The impact of the Yom Kippur War on the IAF: The need for modernization, reorganisation, and a shift to combined arms warfare.
- The IAF's expansion of its mission sets: Deep strike operations, counter-terrorism, and the evolution of UAVs.
- Operation Thunderbolt: The audacious rescue of hostages from Entebbe Airport in Uganda.
- Operation Thunderbolt's impact on the global response to terrorism: A model for future hostage rescue operations.
- The First Lebanon War: The IAF's role in fighting terrorist organizations and the challenges of asymmetric warfare.
- Operation Babylon: The preemptive strike on the Iraqi Osirak nuclear reactor.
- Operation Babylon's impact: A demonstration of the IAF's long-range strike capabilities and its strategic deterrence potential.
- The strike on the PLO HQ in Tunisia: The IAF's continued commitment to fighting terrorism and projecting national power.

Chapter 5: The IAF Today: A Legacy of Innovation and Adaptability

- The two inflection points in IAF history: The impact of Major General Dan Tolkovski and Major General Benny Peled.
- The major factors that have driven the IAF's evolution: Existential threat, intent, air-mindedness of leaders, technology, and quality of personnel.
- The future of the IAF: The challenges of asymmetric warfare, the proliferation of advanced technology, and the need for continued innovation.
- Lessons for other air forces: The IAF's story as a model for how smaller states can build and evolve effective air power.

- Recommendations for further study: The development of a theory to explain the evolution of small state air forces and the importance of contextual factors.

Abstracts

ELI5

This is a book about the Israeli Air Force (IAF), which is like a big group of airplanes that protect Israel. The book is like a story that tells you about how the IAF got started, how it changed over time, and what it's like today.

The IAF started a long time ago when Israel first became a country. At first, they didn't have many airplanes, but they learned how to use them to help the soldiers on the ground.

Over time, the IAF got better and better. They got more airplanes, and they learned how to use them to fight other countries' air forces. They even learned how to fly really far away to attack bad guys in other countries.

Today, the IAF is one of the best air forces in the world. It can fly really fast, it has really powerful weapons, and it can help protect Israel from all kinds of bad guys.

Scientific-Style Abstract

This study examines the evolution of the Israeli Air Force (IAF) from its inception in 1947 to its role as a tool of national power in the 1980s. While previous scholarship on the IAF has focused primarily on descriptive accounts of its operations, this thesis offers a more analytical approach, exploring the factors that shaped the IAF's development.

The research identifies two distinct periods that act as inflection points in the IAF's evolution: the tenures of Major General Dan Tolkovski in the 1950s and Major General Benny Peled in the 1970s. The study further identifies key evolutionary factors that influenced the IAF's development, including:

- **Existential threat and geography:** Israel's small size and constant threat from surrounding Arab states created an urgent need for a capable air force.
- **Intent:** The IAF's mission sets evolved as Israeli leaders developed a more sophisticated understanding of air power's strategic potential.
- **Air-mindedness of leaders:** The vision of key leaders, like Tolkovski and Peled, who understood and championed air power, played a crucial role in shaping the IAF's evolution.
- **Technology and acquisition:** The IAF's rapid modernization through acquisition of advanced aircraft and technology, often from the US, was critical to its development.
- **Divestment of missions and the multirole capability:** The IAF's acquisition of helicopters and unmanned aerial vehicles enabled the reallocation of fighter and bomber resources to strategic missions, emphasizing the multirole capability of the force.

- **Quality and standards:** The IAF's emphasis on rigorous training and high standards for its personnel has been a key factor in its effectiveness.

The study analyzes the impact of major conflicts, including the War of Independence, the Suez Crisis, the Six-Day War, the War of Attrition, and the Yom Kippur War, on the IAF's development. It then explores how the IAF evolved into a strategic force capable of conducting long-range strikes, as demonstrated by operations like Operation Thunderbolt (Entebbe), Operation Babylon (Osirak), and Operation Wooden Leg (PLO headquarters in Tunisia).

This analysis offers valuable insights into the evolution of small state air forces, highlighting the importance of leadership, strategic vision, technological advancement, and the ability to adapt to changing threats. It suggests that even small nations can develop air forces that can project power far beyond their borders and play a significant role in shaping regional and global security dynamics.

Mnemonics

Mnemonic (acronym)

Deterrent **A**irpower **V**isionary **I**ntelligence **D**octrine **S**urvival **W**arfare **I**nnovation **N**ational **G**lobal **S**trategic

Mnemonic (speakable)

David's wings began small, **but Dan** Tolkovski made them strong, **with air** superiority the goal. **Benny Peled** further refined them, **a new** era of strategic air power, **for Israel** to reach out and strike far.

Mnemonic (singable)

(To the tune of "My Bonnie Lies Over the Ocean")

David's wings, so small they were, Fighting hard, for a new land to share. Dan Tolkovski, a new vision took hold, Made them strong, a story to be told.

Benny Peled, he came along, To a new era, of air power strong. From Lebanon to Iraq they flew, Israel's might, for all to view.

From Entebbe to Osirak they struck, A force to be reckoned with, the world they shook. A new era, of strategic might, David's wings, shining ever bright.

Most Important Passages

1. **Page 7, Chapter 1, Introduction:** > "The circumstances surrounding the establishment and existence of the state of Israel are unique within the global context of international history. A relatively new state and objected to from birth, Israel has never had a moment of simple existence. Instead, it has always been preparing to fight or actively fighting for its very existence. The Israeli Defense Forces (IDF) are the instrument of power that has shouldered the burden of these efforts. The Israeli Air Force (IAF) has been the critical key to enabling or ensuring victory and the survival of the state."

This passage sets the stage for the thesis by outlining the unique context of Israel's existence and highlighting the critical role of the IAF in its survival.

2. **Page 9, Chapter 1, Introduction:** > "Despite Israel's underdog status militarily in the Near and Middle East, it survived onslaught after onslaught carried out by its Arab neighbors. Once the survival of the nation became more secure, it did not take long before Israel was projecting its will and power via its Air Force in preemptive attacks or in support of general security and economic measures regionally. The air force had transitioned from a purely reactive and defensive force to one that was able to fulfill strategic military objectives abroad."

This passage introduces the key theme of the thesis: the transformation of the IAF from a defensive force to a strategic instrument of power.

3. **Page 11, Chapter 2, IAF Origins:** > "The origins of the IAF are hurried and crucial to understanding the evolution of the IAF's role and in how Israeli leaders used air power. When the Jews who were living in what was then Palestine understood that the time of the British Mandate was coming to an end, they also knew that resistance to the establishment of Israel as a Jewish state would transform into violent action undertaken by the neighboring Arab nations. When Israel was established, its Air Service consisted of almost no military aircraft designed for combat, but it did exist, albeit with light civilian planes."

This passage emphasizes the unique circumstances of the IAF's creation, highlighting the need for an air force from day one and the challenges of building it in a hostile environment.

4. **Page 16, Chapter 2, Israeli Air Power:** > "The capabilities of the IAF are not merely available number and types of aircraft that were within its inventory. Instead, the personnel, inventory, mission types, and IDF operational requirements need to be explored to understand what capabilities the IAF had. These factors had a synergistic effect of actualizing the IAF's potential."

This passage lays out the key factors that contribute to an air force's capabilities, emphasizing the importance of not just hardware but also personnel, training, and integration within the broader military context.

5. **Page 20, Chapter 2, Operation Yoav:** > "By the end of Operation Yoav, the IAF and its 150 pilots had flown over 239 sorties, dropped 151 tons of bombs, and struck 21 targets, enabling the subsequent IDF control over two-dozen villages in the Negev desert and the surrounding countryside."

This passage showcases the impact of the IAF's actions in Operation Yoav, demonstrating how airpower contributed to strategic objectives and territorial gains.

6. **Page 33, Chapter 3, The Aftermath of the Six-Day War:** > "The new status quo of a post-Six-Day War was problematic for Israel. Although Israel had acquired new land that increased its strategic depth, the IDF was not manned sufficiently to protect and preserve the newly acquired territories of the Sinai, West Bank and Golan. Additionally, the IDF was not designed for the long term, sustainment operations to do so."

This passage highlights the challenges Israel faced after its victory in the Six-Day War, emphasizing the need for a more sustainable and flexible military force.

7. **Page 43, Chapter 4, Introduction:** > "The end of the Yom Kippur War marked a new era for the state of Israel. It would be the last in its history of large force-on-force wars and would represent the dawn of the era of Israeli counterterrorism and asymmetric operations. No longer would Israel's immediate neighbors represent an ongoing existential threat, but rather, with the relative stability that sprouted from the Yom Kippur War ceasefire and negotiations, that threat was now elsewhere."

This passage marks a turning point in Israel's history, showing how the shifting strategic landscape led to the emergence of new threats and a focus on counterterrorism operations.

Page numbering resumes following body of document.

Glossary for Modern Readers

A-4 Skyhawk: A single-seat, carrier-capable, subsonic jet attack aircraft.

Avia S-199: A Czechoslovakian fighter aircraft, based on the German Messerschmitt Bf 109.

Bar Lev Line: A series of Israeli fortifications built along the eastern bank of the Suez Canal.

Beechcraft Bonanza: A single-engine, light aircraft.

Benny Peled: Major General Benny Peled, commander of the IAF from 1969-1973.

CAS: Close Air Support

C-130 Hercules: A four-engine turboprop military transport aircraft.

C-47 Dakota: A twin-engine, military transport aircraft.

Command and Control (C2): The process of directing and coordinating military operations.

Dassault Mirage III: A French supersonic, single-seat fighter aircraft.

Dassault Mystère IV: A French single-engine jet fighter aircraft.

Dassault Ouragan: A French jet-powered fighter bomber.

De Havilland Mosquito: A British twin-engine light bomber aircraft.

Douglas C-47 Dakota: A twin-engine transport aircraft.

Douglas DC-3/C-47 Dakota: A twin-engine transport aircraft.

EAF: Egyptian Air Force

E-2 Hawkeye: An airborne early warning and control aircraft.

El Al Airlines: Israel's national airline.

Entebbe: A town in Uganda, site of the 1976 Entebbe hostage rescue mission.

F-4 Phantom II: A twin-engine, supersonic, multirole combat aircraft.

F-15 Eagle: A twin-engine, supersonic, all-weather, multirole fighter aircraft.

F-16 Fighting Falcon: A single-engine, multirole fighter aircraft.

Force 17: A specialized military unit of the PLO.

Fouga Magister: A French jet-powered trainer aircraft.

Frog Missile: A Soviet-made, short-range, surface-to-surface ballistic missile.

Gloster Meteor: A British jet-powered fighter aircraft.

Haganah: A Jewish paramilitary organization during the British Mandate in Palestine.

Hamas A-Shatt: A suburb of Tunis, Tunisia, site of the 1985 Israeli air raid.

Hawkeye E-2C aircraft: An airborne command, control, and coordination platform that can centrally monitor, deconflict, and direct aircrew and missions from within or near the area of operations.

Hezbollah: A Lebanese Shi'a Islamist political party and militant group.

Hiller UH-12: A single-engine utility helicopter.

IADS: Integrated Air Defense System.

IDF: Israeli Defense Forces

IAF: Israeli Air Force

INF: Israeli Naval Forces

Kfir: A single-seat, Israeli-built jet fighter aircraft.

Kotel: The Western Wall, a holy site for Jewish people.

L-70 Cannon: A Swedish-made towed, anti-aircraft gun.

Lod Airport: A major airport in Israel, later renamed Ben Gurion Airport.

MANPADS: Man-portable air defense system

Mahal: A group of Jewish volunteers from outside Israel who fought in the War of Independence.

MiG-15: A Soviet-made jet fighter aircraft.

Moshe Dayan: Israeli Minister of Defense.

Moshe Dayan: Israeli Minister of Defense, and military leader.

Motta Gur: Chief of Staff of the IDF during the Entebbe hostage rescue mission.

Muki Betser: The deputy commander of Sayeret Matkal during the Entebbe hostage rescue mission.

Operation Babylon: The 1981 Israeli air strike on the Iraqi Osirak nuclear reactor.

Operation Boxer: The 1969 Israeli bombing campaign of Egyptian military positions along the Suez Canal.

Operation Dugman: The 1973 Israeli air strike against Syrian Integrated Air Defense Systems.

Operation Kadesh: The 1956 Israeli military operation during the Suez Canal Crisis.

Operation Moked: The 1967 Israeli preemptive air strike against Arab air forces.

Operation Priha: The 1970 Israeli air campaign against Egyptian military targets.

Operation Tagar: The 1973 Israeli plan to destroy Egyptian and Syrian integrated air defense systems.

Operation Thunderbolt: The 1976 Israeli hostage rescue mission at Entebbe Airport, Uganda.

Operation Wooden Leg: The 1985 Israeli air raid on the PLO headquarters in Tunis, Tunisia.

Osirak: An Iraqi nuclear reactor.

PFLP: Popular Front for the Liberation of Palestine

PLO: Palestinian Liberation Organization

Ras el-Aish: A town on the Egyptian-Israeli border.

Revolutionary Cell: A pro-Palestinian terrorist group.

Sayeret Matkal: A special forces unit of the IDF, also known as "The Unit."

SA-2 Surface-to-Air Missile: A Soviet-made, long-range surface-to-air missile system.

SA-3 Surface-to-Air Missile: A Soviet-made, medium-range, surface-to-air missile system.

SA-6 Surface-to-Air Missile: A Soviet-made, medium-range, mobile surface-to-air missile system.

SA-7 MANPADS: A Soviet-made, short-range, infrared guided surface-to-air missile.

Sabena Flight 571: A passenger airplane hijacked in 1972.

Shimon Peres: Israeli Minister of Defense.

Shrike Missile: An anti-radiation missile.

Skyhawk A-4: A single-seat, carrier-capable, subsonic jet attack aircraft.

Soviet-made 9K52 Luna-M "Frog" Surface-to-Surface Missiles: A Soviet-made, short-range, surface-to-surface ballistic missile.

Super Frelon: A French-built, large, twin-engine, anti-submarine warfare helicopter.

Supermarine Spitfire: A British single-seat, single-engine fighter aircraft.

Sud Vautour II: A French-built, single-seat, attack aircraft.

Suez Canal Crisis: The 1956 international crisis caused by the nationalization of the Suez Canal.

Syrian Air Force: The air force of the Syrian Arab Republic.

Syrian General Command: The headquarters of the Syrian Arab Army.

Tammuz 1: The Osirak nuclear reactor.

Terrorism: The use of violence against civilians for political purposes.

Tolkovski, Dan: Major General Dan Tolkovski, commander of the IAF from 1953-1958.

Tow Missile: A U.S.-made, anti-tank missile.

UAV: Unmanned aerial vehicle

Ugandan Army: The military forces of the Republic of Uganda.

Yasser Arafat: Leader of the PLO.

Yitzhak Rabin: Prime Minister of Israel.

ZSU-23-4 Shilka: A Soviet-made, self-propelled, radar-guided anti-aircraft gun.

Yom Kippur War: The 1973 war between Israel and its Arab neighbors.

Glossary for Lay Readers

Air Power – The ability to leverage the air domain and aviation as a means or way to achieve desired political and military ends.

Al-Naksa – This term translates to "The Setback" and is the term that the Egyptians used to describe the Six-Day War, rather than as an ending. The idea that the war was a setback, not an end, influenced Egyptian actions and operations in the War of Attrition.

Air-mindedness – A mindset of leadership that can conceive of and appropriately implement the power of airpower as a tool or instrument.

Close Air Support (CAS) – A type of airpower in which fixed or rotary wing aircraft are used to support ground forces engaged in combat operations. This is a largely tactical mission set in which aircraft provide kinetic effects to the ground scheme of maneuver.

Command and Control (C2) - Refers to the mechanisms and processes used by the military to organize, direct, and support a military action.

Combined Arms – A military doctrine that advocates for the synchronized actions of all branches of the military, with each supporting and enabling one another to achieve the most desirable effects.

De Havilland DH 98 Mosquito FB6 - An aircraft designed and manufactured in the UK during World War II. This was the main fighter aircraft for the Israeli Air Force (IAF) during the 1950s, though it was considered to be an outdated airframe.

Dassault Ouragan - A jet fighter designed and manufactured in France. This aircraft was one of the first jet fighter aircraft acquired by the IAF during the period of transition into the jet age. It was a multirole aircraft, designed for both bombing and air-to-air combat.

Dassault Mystere IV - A jet fighter designed and manufactured in France. This aircraft was one of the first jet fighter aircraft acquired by the IAF during the period of transition into the jet age. It was a multirole aircraft, designed for both bombing and air-to-air combat.

Dassault Mirage III CJ - A jet fighter designed and manufactured in France. This aircraft was acquired by the IAF in the mid-1960s and represented the IAF's continued transition into the supersonic jet era. It was a highly capable aircraft, capable of both air-to-air and air-to-ground operations.

Electronic Warfare (EW) - The use of electronic systems to detect, identify, and disrupt the enemy's electronic systems. This is a tactic that the IAF leveraged to increase the survivability of its aircraft while operating inside the enemy Integrated Air Defense Systems (IADS).

Electronic Countermeasures (ECM) - The methods and technologies used to disrupt the enemy's use of radar and other electronic systems. ECM is an aspect of Electronic Warfare (EW) that was vital in enabling the IAF's strikes on the Osirak nuclear reactor complex in Iraq.

Entebbe – The site of the airport in Uganda, where the Air France flight was hijacked in 1976. The raid conducted to rescue the hostages by the Israelis was termed Operation Thunderbolt, but is also commonly referred to as Operation Entebbe, for the location of the mission.

Existential Threat - A type of threat that can destroy or severely weaken the state in question.

Force 17 - A specialized unit that operated under the authority of the Palestinian Liberation Organization (PLO) in the 1980s. This unit was responsible for several attacks on Israelis that prompted the Israeli government to strike at the PLO's headquarters in Tunisia in 1985.

Fouga Magister - A jet trainer aircraft designed and manufactured in France. This aircraft was acquired by the IAF in the late 1950s and continued to serve as a trainer aircraft throughout the 1970s and into the 1980s.

F-4 Phantom - A jet fighter designed and manufactured in the US. This aircraft was acquired by the IAF in the late 1960s as part of the IAF's transition to American aircraft. The Phantom was a multirole aircraft and was used in multiple campaigns by the IAF, including the Yom Kippur War.

F-15 Eagle - A jet fighter designed and manufactured in the US. This aircraft was acquired by the IAF in the mid-1970s. It is a highly capable fighter aircraft and is considered to be one of the best air-to-air fighters ever built.

F-16 Fighting Falcon - A jet fighter designed and manufactured in the US. This aircraft was acquired by the IAF in the late 1970s. It is a highly capable fighter aircraft and was used in the air raid against the Osirak nuclear reactor in Iraq.

Gloster Meteor F8 - A jet fighter designed and manufactured in the UK. The IAF acquired this aircraft in the early 1950s during the process of transitioning from propeller-driven aircraft to jets.

Ground Attack - A type of airpower that is used to destroy ground targets.

Ground Troops - The infantry soldiers that make up the ground forces of the IDF.

Guerilla - A type of military strategy that relies on the use of irregular troops to conduct surprise attacks and sabotage against the enemy. Guerilla groups often operate in small, decentralized units.

Hawkeye E-2C - An airborne command and control aircraft designed and manufactured in the US. This aircraft was acquired by the IAF in the mid-1980s to increase the IAF's command and control capabilities for strategic operations.

Hiller UH-12 - A light helicopter designed and manufactured in the US. This aircraft was the first helicopter acquired by the IAF. It was primarily used in a transport role.

Hughes 500 MD Defender - A light helicopter designed and manufactured in the US. This aircraft was acquired by the IAF in the mid-1980s. It was primarily used in a reconnaissance and ground attack role.

Interdiction - The use of airpower to prevent the enemy from moving troops and equipment on the ground.

Integrated Air Defense Systems (IADS) - A complex system of radars, surface-to-air missiles (SAMs), and other air defense assets that are used to protect a country from air attack.

Kfir - A jet fighter designed and manufactured in Israel. This aircraft was based on the French Mirage V aircraft and was developed by Israel Aerospace Industries. The Kfir was a highly capable fighter aircraft and was used in multiple campaigns by the IAF.

Kotel - The Western Wall of the Temple Mount in Jerusalem, which is a holy site for Jews.

Kibbutz – A collective farming community in Israel. The inhabitants of the Kibbutzim often served in the IDF.

Lockheed C-130 Hercules - A transport aircraft designed and manufactured in the US. The C-130 is a very versatile aircraft and was used in multiple campaigns by the IAF. The IAF modified its C-130 aircraft to serve as an aerial refueling tanker.

Lockheed F-104 Starfighter - A supersonic jet fighter designed and manufactured in the US. This aircraft was acquired by the IAF in the late 1950s and was used for air-to-air combat.

Luna-M – A Soviet surface-to-surface ballistic missile system. The Syrians used this system to attack Israeli population centers in the Yom Kippur War.

Mahal Volunteers – Jewish and Zionist volunteers who came to Israel to fight in the War of Independence. These volunteers were often highly trained and experienced pilots and came from various countries across the globe.

MANPADS - Man-portable Air Defense Systems. These are light, easily transportable, passive, infrared-guided systems that do not emit radar signals. This type of system was provided to the Iraqi military to defend the Osirak reactor complex.

MiG-15 - A jet fighter designed and manufactured in the USSR. This aircraft was acquired by the Egyptian Air Force in the 1950s. It was a highly capable fighter aircraft and served as a threat to the IAF for over a decade.

MiG-21 - A jet fighter designed and manufactured in the USSR. This aircraft was acquired by the Egyptian Air Force in the late 1950s and was used for air-to-air combat. The IAF had to upgrade its capabilities to counter this aircraft.

Miles M.57 Aerovan - A transport aircraft designed and manufactured in the UK. This aircraft was acquired by the IAF in the mid-1950s.

Moshe Dayan - A highly influential Israeli military leader who served in many roles for the IDF and Israeli government. Dayan is known for his leadership during the Six-Day War and Yom Kippur War, as well as for his political maneuvering during those conflicts.

Motta Gur - An Israeli military leader who served as the IDF's Chief of Staff during the Yom Kippur War. He was responsible for guiding the IDF's actions in response to the Arab attack.

Multirole - An aircraft capable of conducting a variety of missions.

Nord 2501 Noratlas - A transport aircraft designed and manufactured in France. This aircraft was acquired by the IAF in the late 1950s.

Noorduyn Norseman - A transport aircraft designed and manufactured in Canada. This aircraft was acquired by the IAF in the 1940s. It was used for both transport and bombing.

Osirak - A French-designed nuclear reactor complex that was built in Iraq. The IAF attacked this complex in 1981 in Operation Babylon.

Operation Barbarossa – The invasion of the Soviet Union by Nazi Germany during World War II. Operation Moked, which was the IAF's operation to strike the Egyptian and Syrian air forces in 1967, was modeled after Operation Barbarossa.

Operation Boxer - A bombing campaign conducted by the IAF against Egyptian artillery batteries along the Suez Canal in the War of Attrition.

Operation Dugman - An IAF operation to suppress Syrian Integrated Air Defense Systems (IADS) in the Yom Kippur War.

Operation Freedom Sentinel - An ongoing military operation conducted by the US in Afghanistan.

Operation Freedom Dawn – A military operation conducted by the US in Libya in 2011.

Operation Iraqi Freedom – A military operation conducted by the US in Iraq that began in 2003.

Operation Kadesh – An IDF operation against the Egyptian military in the Suez Canal Crisis in 1956.

Operation Moked – An IDF operation against the Egyptian, Syrian, and Jordanian militaries in the Six-Day War. The operation was a decisive success for the IAF and enabled the IDF's victory in the war.

Operation Odyssey Dawn – A military operation conducted by the US in Libya in 2011.

Operation Priha - A bombing campaign conducted by the IAF against Egyptian military targets in the War of Attrition.

Operation Tagar - A series of IAF operations against Egyptian Integrated Air Defense Systems (IADS) in the Yom Kippur War.

Operation Thunderbolt – An IDF operation conducted to rescue hostages held by pro-Palestinian terrorists at Entebbe Airport in Uganda.

Operation Yoav - An IDF operation against Egyptian ground forces in 1948.

P-51 Mustang - A fighter aircraft designed and manufactured in the US. The IAF acquired this aircraft in the late 1940s.

Palestinian Liberation Organization (PLO) - A political organization that was founded in 1964 with the goal of establishing an independent Palestinian state. The PLO was responsible for multiple terrorist attacks against Israelis.

Popular Front for the Liberation of Palestine (PFLP) - A Palestinian terrorist organization that was founded in 1967. This group was responsible for numerous attacks against Israelis, including the hijacking of an Air France flight in 1976.

Precision-Guided Munitions (PGM) - A type of guided munition that is designed to hit a specific target with great accuracy. PGMs were not used in the air raid against the Osirak nuclear reactor complex, but the Israelis achieved a high level of accuracy in that strike due to careful planning and training.

Ramat David air base - A large air base in northern Israel. This base served as a major hub for the IAF throughout the Arab-Israeli wars.

Ras el-Aish - A small town in Egypt on the eastern bank of the Suez Canal.

Revolutionary Cell - A pro-Palestinian terrorist organization that was involved in the hijacking of an Air France flight in 1976.

Sayeret Matkal - A special forces unit of the IDF known as "The Unit". This unit was responsible for conducting the rescue of the hostages at Entebbe Airport in 1976.

SA-2 surface-to-air missile (SAM) - A surface-to-air missile system designed and manufactured in the USSR. This system was acquired by the Egyptian military and was a major threat to the IAF in the War of Attrition and the Yom Kippur War.

SA-3 surface-to-air missile (SAM) - A surface-to-air missile system designed and manufactured in the USSR. This system was acquired by the Egyptian military and was a major threat to the IAF in the War of Attrition and the Yom Kippur War.

SA-6 surface-to-air missile (SAM) - A surface-to-air missile system designed and manufactured in the USSR. This system was acquired by the Egyptian military in the late 1960s and was a major threat to the IAF in the Yom Kippur War.

SA-7 MANPADS - A man-portable air defense system (MANPADS) designed and manufactured in the USSR. This system was acquired by the Egyptian military and was a major threat to the IAF in the Yom Kippur War.

Sinai Peninsula - A large peninsula located between Egypt and Israel. The peninsula was controlled by Egypt until the Six-Day War in 1967, when it was captured by Israel. Egypt regained control of the Sinai Peninsula in 1979.

Sherut Avir - The precursor to the IAF. This was the air service of the Haganah, which was the Jewish underground organization that fought against the British Mandate in Palestine. The Sherut Avir was responsible for training pilots and preparing for the eventual establishment of Israel.

Skyhawk - A jet fighter designed and manufactured in the US. This aircraft was acquired by the IAF in the late 1960s as part of the IAF's transition to American aircraft.

Supermarine Spitfire - A fighter aircraft designed and manufactured in the UK. This aircraft was acquired by the IAF during the War of Independence. It was a very capable fighter aircraft for the time, though it was soon outmatched by the jets used by the Egyptians.

Strategic Depth - The ability of a country to absorb attack and maintain a fighting force deep behind enemy lines. This is a key component of strategic planning and doctrine.

Strategic Attack – The use of airpower to destroy or degrade a nation-state's ability to wage war, or to affect the political will of its government.

Strategic Effect - The ability of a military operation to achieve a desired outcome at the strategic level, often by influencing political decisionmaking.

Sud Vautour - A jet fighter designed and manufactured in France. The IAF acquired this aircraft in the mid-1960s.

Surface-to-air missile (SAM) - A missile that is launched from the ground to attack aircraft. The IAF had to develop new tactics and technologies to counter the growing capabilities of SAMs.

Syrian Air Forces - The air force of Syria. This force has been a constant threat to Israel since the country's inception and has engaged in air-to-air combat with the IAF in multiple conflicts.

Terrorism - The use of violence against civilian populations to achieve political ends.

The Unit – A common term for the Sayeret Matkal unit, which is a special forces unit of the IDF.

Yitzhak Rabin - An Israeli military leader and politician who served as both the Prime Minister and the Defense Minister of Israel. Rabin played a key role in the negotiations that brought about the peace treaty with Egypt.

Yom Kippur - The Day of Atonement, which is the holiest day in the Jewish year.

ZSU-23 - A self-propelled radar-guided anti-aircraft gun. This system was acquired by the Egyptian military and posed a serious threat to the IAF in the Yom Kippur War.

Index of Persons

Amin, Idi 51, 52, 53

Arafat, Yasser 70, 73

Begin, Menachem 66, 67

Ben-Gurion, David 16, 17, 17

Betser, Muki 51

Bourgiba, Habib 70

Carter, Jimmy 66

Cohen, Eliezer 21, 27, 33, 46, 47, 62, 72, 78

Conversino, Mark iv, iv

Dayan, Moshe 25, 35, 35

Douhet, Giulio 9

Gantz, Benny 75

Goldman, Richard 10, 11, 26, 29, 32, 33, 36, 39, 40, 47, 60

Gordon, Shmuel 10, 21, 26, 27, 28, 29, 30, 31, 32, 33, 34, 35, 36, 37, 38, 39, 40, 41, 43, 44

Gur, Motta 55

Hussein, Saddam 62, 63, 64, 66, 67, 69, 71

Khomeini, Ayatollah 62

Lapidot, Aharon 10, 30

Meir, Golda 31, 35, 35

Mitchell, William "Billy" 5, 86

Mubarak, Hosni 35

Nasser, Gamel Abdel 18, 20, 27, 28, 29, 30, 34, 35, 37, 38, 78

Nasirzadeh, Aziz 1

Netanyahu, Yoni 51

Peled, Benny 5, 46, 48, 52, 53, 54, 55, 56, 57, 58, 59, 61, 62, 71, 78, 82, 83, 84, 87

Peres, Shimon 41, 51, 51, 51, 52, 56, 56, 57, 58, 58, 59, 61, 66, 71, 71, 72, 73, 73, 77

Rabin, Yitzhak 20, 51, 52, 56, 56, 57, 58, 60, 62, 70, 71

Sadat, Anwar 35, 36, 41, 41

Sharon, Ariel 58

Springer, Rita 20

Tolkovski, Dan 5, 16, 16, 17, 18, 18, 19, 20, 21, 22, 23, 23, 24, 25, 26, 27, 29, 30, 43, 45, 46, 52, 53, 54, 78, 82, 83, 84, 86, 87

Watson, Joseph iv

Weidenfeld, Benyamin 52

Zaki, Tahsin 24

Index of Places

A-Shatt, 71, 73, 78

Alley, 59

Al Tawita, 64

Athens, 50

Awali Line, 58

Baghdad, 4, 62, 64, 68, 70, 72, 73, 81

Bhamdoun, 59

Benghazi, Libya, 50

Beirut, Lebanon, 64, 71, 77

Brussels, 50

Cairo, 4, 31, 36, 44, 53, 56

Camp David, 44

Crete, 78

Cyprus, 71, 77

Damascus, 31, 41, 42, 44, 75

El Arish, 14

El-Al Airline, 56

Entebbe, Uganda, 3, 50, 51, 52, 53, 54, 55, 56, 57, 58, 61, 62, 63, 81

Etzion Air Base, 73

France, 18, 19, 50, 53, 54, 57, 64

Galilee, 6, 42

Germany, 57, 58

Goodfellow Air Force Base, Texas, 3

Golan Heights, 26, 42, 44, 75

Great Rift Valley, 6

Hickam AFB, HI, 3

Herzliya, Israel, 13

Isis, 64

Israel, 1, 2, 3, 4, 5, 6, 7, 8, 9, 10, 11, 12, 13, 14, 15, 16, 17, 18, 19, 20, 21, 22, 23, 24, 25, 26, 27, 28, 29, 30, 31, 32, 33, 34, 35, 36, 37, 38, 39, 40, 41, 42, 43, 44, 45, 46, 47, 48, 49, 50, 51, 52, 53, 54, 55, 56, 57, 58, 59, 60, 61, 62, 63, 64, 65, 66, 67, 68, 69, 70, 71, 72, 73, 74, 75, 76, 77, 78, 79, 80, 81, 82, 83, 84, 85, 86, 87

Italy, 78

Jordan, 6, 7, 15, 20, 21, 22, 27, 41, 58, 73

Kampala, 50

Kenya, 54, 55, 56, 57, 58, 61, 63

Larnaca, Cyprus, 71, 77

Langley Air Force Base, Virginia, 3

Lebanon, 7, 28, 58, 59, 64, 71, 77, 81

Lod Airport, 50, 53, 56, 61, 63

London, 18

Luna-M "Frog", 40

Manhattan College, 3

Maxwell Air Force Base, Alabama, 2

Mediterranean Sea, 6, 11, 50, 70, 71, 78, 79

Migdal HaEmek, 40

Miles M.57 Aerovan, 20

Mogadishu, 57

Moscow, 31, 29

Motta Gur, 56

Negev Desert, 6, 14, 31, 37, 42

New Jersey, 6

New York City, 3

New York University, 3

Nord 2501 Noratlas, 20

Ofira Air Base, 62

Osirak, 62, 64, 69, 70, 72, 73, 81, 87

Paris, 50

Palestinian Authority, 7

Peled, Benny, 3, 44, 52, 53, 54, 56, 57, 61, 75, 78, 81, 83, 85, 86

Port Said, 30

Port Tawfik, 30

Ramat David Air Base, 40, 41

Ras el-Aish, 30

Revolution Cell, 50

River Jordan, 6

RWD-13, 12

Sabena Airline, 50, 51

Samarian Hills, 6

Saudi Arabia, 73

Sayeret Matkal, 50

Sofar, 59

Suez Canal, 18, 19, 20, 25, 28, 29, 30, 31, 34, 36, 37, 38, 40, 42, 44, 46, 47, 75

Syria, 6, 7, 11, 15, 21, 22, 25, 27, 28, 29, 30, 31, 32, 34, 35, 37, 38, 39, 40, 41, 42, 44, 48, 58, 59, 64, 75, 83, 84

Taylorcraft Model C, 12

Tel Aviv, 50

Tunisia, 3, 70, 71, 77, 81

Uganda, 3, 50, 51, 52, 53, 54, 55, 56, 57, 58, 61, 63, 81

USSR, 28, 29, 31, 35, 36, 40, 62, 64, 79

West Bank, 7, 26, 44

Westwing, 60

Vienna, 50

Yom Kippur War, 4, 25, 29, 30, 31, 32, 33, 34, 35, 36, 37, 38, 39, 40, 41, 42, 43, 44, 45, 46, 47, 48, 49, 51, 52, 53, 54, 55, 60, 71, 75, 77, 79, 81, 83, 84, 85, 86

Yemen, 28

Zaki, Tahsin, 24

ZSU-23, 40

Innovative Indexes based on "David's Wings: The Strategic Development of the Israeli Air Force"

Index 1: Evolutionary Factors and Inflection Points

- **Air-mindedness of Leaders:** Examines the role of vision and understanding of airpower in shaping the IAF.
    - **Dan Tolkovski:** The impact of his vision on IAF modernization and standardization (Chapter 2).
    - **Benny Peled:** Post-Yom Kippur War reforms and shift towards a more strategically-oriented IAF (Chapter 4).
- **Existential Threat and Geography:** Analyzes the impact of Israel's unique geopolitical situation on IAF development.
    - **Strategic Depth:** The lack of strategic depth and its implications on IAF doctrine and capabilities (Chapters 2, 3, & 4).
    - **Proximity of Threats:** How the close proximity of adversaries initially influenced IAF missions and capabilities (Chapters 2 & 3).
- **Technology and Acquisition:** Traces the IAF's acquisition of aircraft and technology, and its impact on doctrine and capability.
    - **Standardization Efforts:** Tolkovski's emphasis on equipment standardization (Chapter 2).
    - **Modernization:** Post-Yom Kippur War acquisition of advanced aircraft and technology (Chapter 4).
- **Divestment of Missions and Multirole Capability:** Examines the impact of new technologies and aircraft on mission sets and the IAF's ability to perform multiple roles.
    - **Helicopters and UAVs:** Their introduction and impact on IAF doctrine and operational capabilities (Chapter 4).
- **Quality and Standards:** Focuses on the IAF's commitment to high-quality personnel, rigorous training, and a culture of excellence.
    - **Training Programs:** The length and intensity of IAF pilot training programs (Chapter 5).
    - **Washout Rates:** High washout rates as evidence of IAF's commitment to quality (Chapter 5).

Index 2: Major Operations and Campaigns

- **Operation Yoav:** Israel's first offensive operation in the War of Independence (Chapter 2).
- **Operation Kadesh:** The Suez Canal Crisis and its impact on IAF doctrine and capabilities (Chapter 2).
- **Operation Moked:** The preemptive strike against Arab air forces in the Six-Day War (Chapter 2).
- **War of Attrition:** The period of limited conflict following the Six-Day

War (Chapter 3).
- **Operation Priha:** The first offensive air strikes by the IAF against Egyptian targets in the War of Attrition (Chapter 3).
- **Yom Kippur War:** The 1973 war and its impact on IAF doctrine and capabilities (Chapter 3).
- **Operation Thunderbolt:** The raid on Entebbe Airport to rescue hostages (Chapter 4).
- **First Lebanon War:** Israel's involvement in the Lebanese Civil War and the use of airpower against terrorist organizations (Chapter 4).
- **Operation Babylon:** The preemptive strike against the Osirak nuclear reactor in Iraq (Chapter 4).
- **Operation Wooden Leg:** The Israeli airstrike against the PLO headquarters in Tunisia (Chapter 4).

Index 3: Key Themes and Concepts

- **Air Superiority:** Examines the IAF's quest for air superiority and its role in Israeli strategy.
    - **Preemptive Strikes:** The IAF's use of preemptive strikes to achieve air superiority (Chapters 2, 3, & 4).
    - **Electronic Warfare:** The IAF's reliance on electronic warfare to counter enemy air defenses (Chapters 3 & 4).
- **Combined Arms Warfare:** Analyzes the evolution of IAF doctrine from a focus on ground support to combined arms operations.
    - **Integration of Airpower:** The IAF's role in supporting ground forces and achieving strategic objectives (Chapters 2, 3, & 4).
    - **Interservice Cooperation:** The evolution of cooperation between the IAF and IDF ground forces (Chapter 4).
- **Strategic Deterrence:** Explores the IAF's role in deterring potential adversaries through its capabilities and operations.
    - **Nuclear Deterrence:** The role of Israel's nuclear program in deterring Arab aggression (Chapters 3 & 4).
    - **Conventional Deterrence:** The use of airpower to deter terrorism and aggression (Chapters 4 & 5).
- **Counterterrorism:** Examines the IAF's role in combating terrorism and its impact on the global landscape of counterterrorism.
    - **Long-Range Strikes:** The IAF's ability to conduct long-range strikes against terrorist targets (Chapters 4 & 5).
    - **Strategic Messaging:** The use of airpower to communicate Israel's resolve against terrorism (Chapters 4 & 5).
- **Evolution of Air Power:** Analyzes the factors that contributed to the IAF's transformation from a tactical force to a strategic instrument of national power.
    - **Inflection Points:** The periods of major change and reform within the IAF (Chapters 2, 3, & 4).
    - **Lessons Learned:** The impact of war and conflict on IAF doctrine,

capabilities, and strategy (Chapters 2, 3, & 4).

Timeline

May 14, 1948: The state of Israel is established, and the Sherut Avir formally transitions to the Israeli Air Force (IAF).

May 25, 1948: The first military aircraft purchases begin to arrive, and the first Douglas C-47 transport plane is made operational in Israel.

May 27, 1948: The IAF formally transitions from the Sherut Avir (Air Service) to the official Israeli Air Force as a part of the establishment of the Israel Defense Forces (IDF).

May 29, 1948: The first four Israeli fighter aircraft, Czech Avia S-199 fighters, take to the skies for a combat mission.

June 4, 1948: The first Israeli Fairchild aircraft is lost during a bombing raid against enemy ground forces.

June 7, 1981: Eight IAF F-16 aircraft dropped sixteen 2,000-pound weapons on Iraq's nuclear reactor, reducing it to rubble in two minutes.

October 6, 1973: The Egyptian and Syrian armies conduct their coordinated opening gambits and strike at Israel.

October 9, 1973: Syrian ground forces launch Soviet-made 9K52 Luna-M "Frog" surface-to-surface missiles, landing in Migdal HaEmek in Northern Israel, close to the Syrian border.

October 22, 1973: A ceasefire is declared after 16 days of the Yom Kippur War.

June 27, 1976: Two Popular Front for the Liberation of Palestine (PFLP) members and two Revolutionary Cell members hijack an Air France flight to Paris from Israel via Athens.

July 3, 1976: The fully laden Hercules airplanes take off from Lod airport to launch Operation Thunderbolt.

July 4, 1976: The rescued hostages land in Lod Airport after Operation Thunderbolt.

September 30, 1980: The Iranian Air Force attempts a strike at the Iraqi nuclear reactor complex.

October 1, 1985: The ten-ship formation of Israeli F-15 fighter aircraft launch Operation Wooden Leg.

October 2, 1985: An Israeli air raid destroys Yasser Arafat's base in Tunisia.

DAVID'S WINGS:

THE STRATEGIC DEVELOPMENT OF THE ISRAELI AIR FORCE

BY

LT COL KELLY "KGB" BORUKHOVICH

A THESIS PRESENTED TO THE FACULTY OF

THE SCHOOL OF ADVANCED AIR AND SPACE STUDIES

FOR COMPLETION OF GRADUATION REQUIREMENTS

SCHOOL OF ADVANCED AIR AND SPACE STUDIES

AIR UNIVERSITY

MAXWELL AIR FORCE BASE, ALABAMA

JUNE 2019

DISTRIBUTION A. Approved for public release: distribution unlimited.

APPROVAL

The undersigned certify that this thesis meets master's-level standards of research, argumentation, and expression.

_____

DR. MARK CONVERSINO   (Date)

_____

DR. SEAN BRANIFF   (Date)

DISCLAIMER

The conclusions and opinions expressed in this document are those of the author. They do not reflect the official position of the US Government, Department of Defense, the United States Air Force, or Air University.

ABOUT THE AUTHOR

Lieutenant Colonel Kelly "KGB" Borukhovich was born and raised in New York City and graduated from New York University where she commissioned through the ROTC program at Manhattan College in 2004. Upon receiving her commission, she completed the fundamentals of intelligence courses at Goodfellow Air Force Base, Texas. Her first operational assignment was to the 613th Air and Space Operation Center in Hickam AFB, HI. Lieutenant Colonel Borukhovich has experience at the squadron, group, headquarters, and joint levels with wartime and contingency experience in Operation Iraqi Freedom, Operation Odyssey Dawn, Operation Enduring Freedom, and Operation Freedom Sentinel. She has been selected to command the 27th Intelligence Squadron at Langley Air Force Base, Virginia.

ACKNOWLEDGEMENTS

I would like to acknowledge the people without whose support and guidance I would not have completed this thesis and year of study. First, to my classmates who humble and inspire me daily with insightful and wise comments beyond our years. Second, to the entire faculty and staff of the School of Advanced Air and Space Studies, my sincerest thanks in fielding my questions, mentoring me in my writing, and guiding my lines of inquiry and thought to new levels. I can sincerely say I am a better person, officer, and leader because of all of you.

I especially want to thank Dr. Mark Conversino for the many lengthy discussions regarding SAASS, thesis, studies, officership, and life. His thought-provoking words pushed my habits of mind and patterns of inquiry to new levels, allowing me to explore course and thesis topics more deeply. Additionally, I would like to thank Lieutenant Colonel Joseph Watson for believing in me and pushing me to attend SAASS.

Most importantly, I cannot fully express my gratitude to my spouse and our child, for their love, patience, support, and understanding when we had to sacrifice time as a family so that I could read, study, or write. This thesis and my achievements are as much do to their discipline and persistence as much as my own. If it were not for my wife holding down the fort, I would not have successfully completed the school year.

ABSTRACT

Although much has been written documenting the 72 years of the Israeli Air Force's (IAF) existence and operations, most have been mostly descriptive rather than analytical. Little has been written that explores the evolution of the IAF as a tool of national strategy. This thesis broadly traces the evolution of the IAF from its inception in 1947 to its modern state, including its capabilities, missions, visions, and roles as an instrument of military and national strategy. The thesis seeks to answer the central question of what factors have influenced the evolution of the IAF from 1947 to the present? Through a historical narrative of the IAF, the analysis highlights two distinct periods that act as inflection points in the IAF development, the tenures of Major General Dan Tolkovski in the 1950s and Major General Benny Peled in the 1970s. Additionally, it identifies evolutionary factors that contribute to the degree of evolution and change within the IAF's history. They are existential threat and geography, intent, air-mindedness of leaders, technology and acquisition, divestment of missions and the multirole mission, and quality and standards. The exploration of the evolution of the IAF in the context of its geopolitical circumstances offers the opportunity to better understand the ways in which small states' air forces can evolve. This examination highlights the inflection points, timing, and factors that directly influenced the evolution and development of the IAF as both an air power and ultimately as a tool of national power.

CONTENTS

Chapter   Page

Disclaimer………………………………………………………………………..……...ii
About the Author………………………………………………………………..…….…iii
Acknowledgments………………………………………………………………..….…..iv
Abstract…………………………………………………………………..……………….v

1   Introduction……………………………………………………………..…….…1
2   David's Wings, The Birth of the Israeli Air Force, 1948-1967……………...........9
3   David's Sky, 1967-1973………………………………………..…...…..............25
4   David's Reach, A New Era as an Instrument of Power, 1973-1985…..………...44
5   Implications and Conclusion……………………………….…..……………….75
6   Bibliography……..……………………………………….……………………..89

Illustrations

Table 1. *Sherut Avir* inventory at the end of the British Mandate, May 14, 1948….12
Table 2. IAF operational inventory on the eve of Operation Yoav …………….…...14
Table 3. IAF operational inventory on the eve of Operation Moked, 1 June 1967….22
Table 4. IAF operational inventory for the month of June 1967……………….…...26
Table 5. IAF operational inventory in October 1973……………………….……….36
Table 6. IAF starting inventory in 1978……………………………………………..60

Chapter 1

Introduction

Iran was growing impatient to fight Israel and promised to destroy the "Zionist regime...The young people in the air force are fully ready and impatient to confront the Zionist regime and eliminate it from the Earth.

Brig. Gen. Aziz Nasirzadeh
Head of the Iranian Air Force

Introduction

The circumstances surrounding the establishment and existence of the state of Israel are unique within the global context of international history. A relatively new state and objected to from birth, Israel has never had a moment of simple existence. Instead, it has always been preparing to fight or actively fighting for its very existence. The Israeli Defense Forces (IDF) are the instrument of power that has shouldered the burden of these efforts. The Israeli Air Force (IAF) has been the critical key to enabling or ensuring victory and the survival of the state.

In its critical role in defending the state, the IAF presents an interesting case study. Unlike many countries that possess premier air forces, Israel joined the aerial domain of war late, cultivating an underground air force after World War II, and formally establishing its Air Force on the first day of its independence. Other major and minor powers were able to cultivate and grow their air forces in line with advancing technologies following the end of the first World War. Thus, the air-mindedness of their military and civic leaders was able to evolve as the aircraft evolved, ingraining it into their psyches with institutional and personal experience in war and conflict. Additionally, European nations were thus able to grow their air forces incrementally, often during periods of peace – e.g., 1919-1939 – through limited 'experimentation' such as the Spanish Civil war, and leverage organizational momentum to continuously evolve their air forces, acquiring and integrating new technologies. Lastly, this also led to the rise of domestic aircraft industries that fed the military appetite for more modern, faster, stronger, and better military aircraft.

On the other hand, Israel required a working air force for the defense of its existence, from the very day that the state came into being. The near-constant existential threat, time, necessity, and lack of strategic depth shaped the evolution of the IAF and created the conditions of its operations. These conditions initially restricted the IAF's operations to local, regional, and relatively tactical planning and operations for decades.

The Modernized IAF

Despite Israel's underdog status militarily in the Near and Middle East, it survived onslaught after onslaught carried out by its Arab neighbors. Once the survival of the nation became more secure, it did not take long before Israel was projecting its will and power via its Air Force in preemptive attacks or in support of general security and economic measures regionally. The air force had transitioned from a purely reactive and defensive force to one that was able to fulfill strategic military objectives abroad. Within three decades of its establishment, IAF operations were answering national strategic requirements such as executing the Entebbe rescue mission and striking Iraqi nuclear reactors.

In strictly military terms, the IAF's mission sets started small and focused on the battlefield, expanding with each new accomplishment. In its beginnings, the IAF's leaders understood that the technical limitations of their aircraft inventory placed it in a role that allowed only support of ground operations and Command and Control (C2) decisions. Likewise, defeat in ground combat would mean a defeat for the nation. The initial acquisition of military-grade aircraft following independence allowed the IAF to expand its missions to include air superiority and interdiction. Subsequent IAF technological revolutions carried the force into the jet and precision-guided munition age. This technologically-enabled increase in capability allowed IAF planners to conceive of missions and effects that could answer broader national strategy challenges.

The Israeli understanding of and reliance on more capable air power grew with every battle and operation. In the first quarter century of its existence, the IAF partook in no less than five major wars or campaigns, each one serving as another data point for improvement in doctrine, tactics, and technology. The Israelis underwent a fundamental pivot in air-mindedness in the 1970s that manifested itself in the modernized inventory and utilization of the IAF as a tool of national power.

This pivot enabled four significant operations to take place that would have been previously impossible, the air raid on the Syrian General Command; the rescue mission in

Entebbe, Uganda; the raid on the Iraqi nuclear reactor; and the strike at the Palestinian Liberation Front headquarters in Tunisia. The raid on the Iraqi nuclear reactor was the most impressive of them all from a purely air power perspective. While the other three operations represented impressive strike and mobility capabilities separately, the nuclear reactor raid represented the comprehensive modernization and premiere capability of the IAF as a tool of strategic importance. It also demonstrated that following a little more than three decades of Independence, Israel leaders had developed a strategic airmindedness.

On June 7, 1981, IAF F-16 aircraft conducted an attack against the nuclear reactor "Tammuz 1" located in southern Baghdad. The operation was the culmination of a year of preparation by the IAF's intelligence forces and resources. To support this mission, IAF intelligence forces had to gather the information surrounding the target itself but also had to satisfy requirements to ensure the survivability of the aircraft taking part in the mission. This strike represented the longest-range strike to date for the IAF, taking it outside of its "comfort zone" of operating against immediate neighbors to regionally significant strikes across the Middle East. The distance presented challenges to intelligence collection to feed the planning process, and it was only the deliberate action of a mature intelligence force that enabled the success of the mission.

All these considerations exacerbated the difficulty that the mission meant to the intelligence collection and exploitation system.[1] The IAF intelligence worked diligently for a year, collecting, exploiting, and translating information into intelligence as they examined threats along the route, as well as the target itself in order to time the strike such that the attack would occur just before the activation of the reactor. The raid on the Tammuz 1 embodied the strategic capacity of the planning and action arms of the IAF. The risks associated with this mission were numerous, and every day offered the potential of a leak that would undermine the entire planning effort. Ultimately, eight IAF F-16 aircraft dropped sixteen 2,000-pound weapons on Iraq's nuclear reactor, reducing it to rubble in two minutes.[2] Not only was the strike force able to escape detection en-route to the target and back, but the entire operation was planned with surgical precision. The strike occurred

---

[1] Aharon Lapidot, ed., *Open Skies* שמיים נקיים*: The Israeli Air Force: 40 Years* (Tel Aviv, Israel: Israeli Ministry of Defense and Peli Press, 1998), 91.
[2] David Rodman, *Sword and Shield of Zion : The Israel Air Force in the Arab-Israeli Conflict, 1948-2012* (Portland, OR: Sussex Academic Press, 2013), 57.

just before the reactor became operational, avoiding possible radioactive fallout.[3] The implications of this attack would not be fully understood until the onset of the 1991 Gulf War in which Iraqi SCUD missiles were being launched at U.S. and coalition forces, as well as at Israel itself, but, significantly, without nuclear warheads.

Sources

The literature focusing on the IAF's role in Israeli conflict, war, and current events is limited, and thus this thesis draws heavily from several sources (e.g., Rubenstein and Goldman, Dunstan, Gordan, and Bar-Joseph) in depicting the historical narrative. Broadly, the literature falls into three categories; as an auxiliary to the ground forces' role in the war, the utilization of the IAF in pursuit of air superiority, or histories of the IAF focusing on battles, personal stories, and aircraft inventory. This thesis differs from the previous works on the IAF by interweaving the narratives, operational conflicts, and tactical examination to draw larger conclusions about the importance of the events and factors within the IAF history that contributed to its evolution from a tactical force to a strategic tool of national power.

The history of the IAF sits in the middle of a largely debated and volatile international relations topic. The very existence of the state of Israel polarizes people and academics alike. As such, it is difficult to find sources that are written objectively and without bias for either the Israeli or Arab causes. Thus, all sources of information for this thesis will be evaluated, considering the sensitivity of this topic. This thesis does not support the validity of either the Israeli or Arab claim but instead focuses on the use of the IAF in the regional and global context in which it became a strategic tool.

Problem Statement

Although much has been written documenting the 72 years of the Israeli Air Force's existence and operations, most have been mostly descriptive rather than analytical. Little has been written that explores the evolution of the IAF as a tool of national strategy. This thesis will broadly trace the evolution of the IAF from its inception in 1947 to its current state, including its capabilities, missions, visions, and roles as an instrument of military and national strategy. This thesis will seek to answer the central question of what factors have influenced the evolution of the Israeli Air Force from 1947 to the present?

---

[3] Lapidot, *Open Skies* שמיים נקיים: *The Israeli Air Force: 40 Years*, 8.

As one of the more capable air forces in the world, a deeper understanding of the IAF's evolution and its role today as a national instrument of power will inform US Airmen on how to best capitalize on its combined operations with Israel as an ally, and focus our assessments of its capabilities and future employment. Additionally, as a relevant study to other geographically small states, this serves as a case study as to whether the evolution of the IAF and its accomplishments were unique to Israel, or are there lessons that other small but technically advanced states could adopt to evolve their air power arms.

Definitions

Air power has been defined in numerous ways by scholars of military operations and strategy. General William "Billy" Mitchell defined air power is defined as the ability to do something in the air.[4] This thesis defines air power in the military sense as the ability to leverage the air domain and aviation as a means or way to achieve desired political and military ends.

In the nuclear era, the US has made the concept of strategic attack synonymous to a nuclear strike against strategic targets. Strategic attack also has a conventional aspect of attacking targets with strategic value. This thesis will utilize 'strategic attack' in terms of using conventional weapons and attack in pursuit of strategic effect.

Geography

The state of Israel is comprised of four geographic areas: a fertile, flat set of coastal plains along the coastline of the Mediterranean Sea; a ridgeline of rolling hills splitting the country, including the central Samarian hills and the hills of Galilee in the north; the long Great Rift Valley runs north to south to the Gulf of Aqaba; and the Negev Desert dominates the southern portion of the country. The River Jordan forms a natural border (and is the sole buffer) between Israel and Jordan (a former and potential future adversary).[5] The country is not wealthy in natural resources and even has had to fight for the very resources that allow for life in the desert: agricultural land and water.

Israel is geospatially located in a place which creates a complex operating environment. Israel is a small country, roughly the size of the state of New Jersey, and is

---

[4] William Mitchell, *Winged Defense : The Development and Possibilities of Modern Air Power--Economic and Military* (Tuscaloosa, AL: University of Alabama Press, 2009), xii.
[5] "World Atlas, Geography of Israel," accessed December 4, 2018, https://www.worldatlas.com/webimage/countrys/asia/israel/illand.htm.

surrounded on three sides by nations that have at one time desired or currently desire its obliteration. On the fourth side is a sea that its enemies can utilize to attack or threaten Israeli assets and trade. Regionally, Israel is surrounded by Arab and Muslim states, sharing its borders from north to south with Lebanon, Jordan, the Palestinian Authority ruling the West Bank, and Egypt. The encirclement does not stop at just these four but instead extends outwards well into the Asian and North Africa continents. From Israel's perspective, it has sworn enemies as far as the eye can see in almost all cardinal directions.

The influence of this small nation surrounded by Goliath adversaries, cannot be underestimated. Without strategic depth as a nation, it meant that any loss, failure, or concession could result in an unacceptable lack of security for the nation writ large. Thus, any threat had only a small buffer until it crossed the threshold into an existential threat. This threat escalation possibility placed increased emphasis within civil and military leader's decisions as they acted in the interest of the survival of the state, every time.

The IAF Today

Today, the IAF is an integral part of the Israeli Defense Forces. In many mission types and scenarios, it represents the vanguard of the force. Israeli political and military leadership has purposely developed and advanced the IAF technologically to ensure its success in original mission sets of defense of the country and support of ground troops but has also expanded the force to a wider variety of missions that demonstrate its utility as a tool of national power. The Israeli Air Force publicly states its mission as inclusive of the following tasks:

> To protect the state of Israel and the IDF's theaters of operation from aerial attacks
> To achieve aerial superiority in all of the IDF's theaters of operation
> To provide air support for both the ground and the naval forces
> To attack targets deep in enemy territory
> To help create a comprehensive concept of aerial intelligence for the air force, and assist the IDF's Intelligence Division
> To transport troops, equipment and weapon systems
> To carry out SAR and extraction missions
> To perform special operations
> To continually build and improve itself, as part of the general plan to improve the entire IDF[6]

---

[6] "The Israeli Air Force, Mission Statement," accessed December 4, 2018, http://www.iaf.org.il/34-en/IAF.aspx.

This broad but explicit array of missions demonstrates the nation's air-mindedness and ability to utilize airpower. As this thesis will show, unlike many conflicts that air forces have encountered in their infancies and evolution, there was little in the way of interservice rivalry, vying for power between the air force and the IDF ground forces. Interservice power struggles would be petty in light of an existential threat, which is what the IDF felt it faced daily. Although the IAF did experience growing pains, the prioritization of ground priorities was more a matter of civil leaders' lack of airmindedness, than that of a rivalry.

Methodology and Structure

In examining the collected information on the IAF's evolution, missions, and purposes, this thesis aims to identify the historical inflection points and factors that changed the direction and use of the IAF as a tool of national power. Sources on the Israeli Air Force are not abundant but are sufficient to answer these baseline research questions. Such sources include historical books and research on the early decades of IDF/IAF operations, works examining the suppression of Integrated Air Defense System (IADS), close air support, air superiority operations, and finally, research exploring Israeli national objectives during those events. Sources will also include periodicals, Israeli civilian and military leader commentary during those significant historical events as well as the IDF/IAF's own Public Affairs' publications on operational history, in both the source language and in English. The research will be judged as to its uniqueness to Israel's situation or if the IAF's experience is universally applicable to larger countries' air forces' development. Finally, if indeed unique to Israel a small state, the research will try to glean lessons learned and unique variables that can be derived from its evolution that can be applied to other small countries.

This thesis will take a mostly chronological approach in examining the IAF's evolution. Chapters two through four will focus on a single theme or historical period each. Chapter two will cover the period from approximately 1948 to 1967 and the early Arab-Israeli Wars. This chapter will also explore the first evolution in the IAF, bringing the force into the jet age. Along with examining the new aircraft capabilities, this chapter will show the expansion of the IAF mission set from CAS to air superiority and interdiction. Chapter three will cover the 1967 to 1973 period, focusing on the Yom Kippur War and the War of Attrition. This period provided experiences that drove the way the IAF conducted its missions, assessed the value of capabilities, and how it planned future force-on-force operations.

Additionally, this chapter will show the budding defense relationship between the US and Israel. Chapter four will cover the period after the Yom Kippur war, approximately 1973 to 1985. This will include the introduction of air power against asymmetric or state-sponsored threats, the influence of attaining "de facto nuclear state" status on its operations, and the continued US military and defense support. Moreover, it will cover the last major technological revolution in its aircraft and capabilities in the mid-1980s, the expansion of its mission sets to include conventional deep strategic attack, and the IAF's modern use as a tool of national power. Chapter five will provide a brief summary of the thesis and tie it together with any findings and conclusions. Also, this chapter will outline recommended further research topics to build further on the research presented within the thesis.

Preliminary Findings

The historical narrative of the IAF highlights two distinct periods that act as inflection points in the IAF development, the tenures of Major General Dan Tolkovski in the 1950s and Major General Benny Peled in the 1970s. Additionally, the analysis identifies evolutionary factors that contribute to the degree of evolution and change within the IAF's history. They are existential threat and geography, intent, air-mindedness of leaders, technology and acquisition, divestment of missions and the multirole mission, and quality and standards. These inflection points and evolutionary factors are discussed further in Chapter Five.

Summary

The exploration of the evolution of the IAF in the context of its geopolitical circumstances offers the opportunity to better understand the ways in which small states' air forces can evolve. This examination highlights the inflection points, timing, and factors that directly influenced the evolution and development of the IAF as both an air power and ultimately as a tool of national power.

Chapter 2

David's Wings, The Birth of the Israeli Air Force, 1948-1967

I have always maintained that the essential purpose of an Air Force is to conquer the command of the air by first wiping out the enemy's air forces.

- General Giulio Douhet

The period from 1948 to 1967 includes the early Arab Israeli Wars and demonstrates the Israeli Air Force's (IAF) transition from a reactionary to a preparatory force. This chapter will briefly examine the IAF from before its inception, through the trial by fire of the war of independence, and into the period of relative peace that allowed it to prepare for the Sinai Campaign and the Six Day War. Additionally, it focuses on the initial changes in the IAF's acquisition and inventory strategies as it entered the jet age. This chapter will show that along with new aircraft capabilities, the IAF expanded its mission sets from Close Air Support (CAS) and reconnaissance to air superiority and interdiction.

IAF Origins

The origins of the IAF are hurried and crucial to understanding the evolution of the IAF's role and in how Israeli leaders used air power. When the Jews who were living in what was then Palestine understood that the time of the British Mandate was coming to an end, they also knew that resistance to the establishment of Israel as a Jewish state would transform into violent action undertaken by the neighboring Arab nations. When Israel was established, its Air Service consisted of almost no military aircraft designed for combat, but it did exist, albeit with light civilian planes.

Under the British Mandate, the fetal state of Israel was not able to purchase nor acquire aircraft for an air force because it was not yet seen as a valid buyer as an independent foreign state.[1] As such, Israel could not purchase fighters, bombers, or cargo planes. Instead, the IAF began its training and recruitment as a shadow/underground air force by establishing flying clubs and through the third-party acquisitions of aircraft. Additionally, many countries hesitated to demonstrate solidarity with and support for a country which was under threat from its neighbors before it had even established its independence, particularly when they those same countries held standing agreements and treaties with her Arab neighbors.[2] Instead, Jews living in Israel purchased light civilian airplanes, which served as military trainers and reconnaissance aircraft at the onset of the

---

[1] Murray Rubenstein and Richard Goldman, *Shield of David* (Englewood-Cliffs, New Jersey: Prentice-Hall, 1978), 15.
[2] Rubenstein and Goldman, 15.

war of independence.³ Other supporters of Israel acquired aircraft abroad and readied them to be smuggled into the fledgling state. The *Sherut Avir* had a laughable starting inventory on the eve of the declaration of its independence as depicted in Table 1, and the threat outside its borders loomed large. The continuous presence of a looming threat is a situation to which Israel would long become accustomed.

The modern state of Israel has never existed without an existential threat lingering just outside its borders. This constant threat created a different lens through which to interpret the world and the region's events. Through this lens, any threat must be answered with any and all resources available, often in less than ideal situations and with less than adequate resources and assets. This creates an interesting contrast in the utilization of available assets versus perfect circumstances and uses, as spelled out in modern theories and doctrine. When facing an existential threat, there may be no other options than working with what one has at that moment, as Israel demonstrated by using every functioning flying vehicle during the war of independence. Thus, it is essential to examine the specific capabilities of the IAF at different points in time to understand the options that were available to senior IDF/IAF and civilian leaders.

Israeli Air Power

The capabilities of the IAF are not merely available number and types of aircraft that were within its inventory. Instead, the personnel, inventory, mission types, and IDF operational requirements need to be explored to understand what capabilities the IAF had. These factors had a synergistic effect of actualizing the IAF's potential.

Again, the precursor to the IAF was the *Sherut Avir* (שירות אוויר) or Air Service that was manned and operated by the Jewish underground in the last years of the British Mandate. The *Sherut Avir* as part of the *Haganah,* or Defense, had practiced its application of airpower as part of the guerilla attacks on the British as well as in defense against Arab incursions into Jewish-owned lands.⁴ The *Haganah* was an underground paramilitary force during the time of the British Mandate in Palestine that would later form the core of the IDF. However, the *Sherut Avir* was nothing close to the Air Force that would be needed to facilitate the overall defense of the nation against those who would crush them. The *Sherut*

---

³ Rubenstein and Goldman, 13–18.
⁴ Rubenstein and Goldman, 15.

Avir was composed of any air-minded individuals who had pursued either flying or maintenance roles independently or as part of their secret assignment from the *Haganah* in preparation for the Israeli Independence Day and expected conflict. Israel and Zionism inspired many outside the British Mandate to support the fight for Israeli existence, and foreign wealthy or well-placed individuals made it their mission to supply the IDF in whatever way possible. For example, two Beechcraft Model 35 Bonanza aircraft were delivered to the IAF by external supporters of the defense and establishment of the state of Israel.[5]

In Early summer 1948, 20 American Piper Cubs arrived in Israel.[6] These aircraft would later be used in observation and bombardment roles. The aircraft inventory of the *Sherut Avir* on the eve of its transformation into the IAF was not that of a formidable airpower nation. Table 1 shows the meager twenty-eight aircraft that Israel controlled when it transitioned the *Sherut Avir* into the IAF on its Independence Day. Under the British Mandate, the Jews were unable to purchase any military aircraft. It was initially only through the authorized areo clubs that the Haganah acquired aircraft. Thus, the inventory consisted of all light civilian aircraft of various sizes and speeds. However, that did not limit the IAF's ingenuity when applying that available airpower to the military environment. Although these aircraft were not designed for military operations, the IAF planners and pilots were able to find applications that successfully supported the IDF in its defense of the new state.

---

[5] Rubenstein and Goldman, 20.
[6] Rubenstein and Goldman, 18.

Table 1. *Sherut Avir* inventory at the end of the British Mandate, May 14, 1948.

Aircraft Model	Aircraft Type / Utilized Role	Number of Aircraft
Austers (A.O.P. 5 and J/1 Autocrat)	Light aircraft/ observation plane	19
Noorduyn Norseman	Light aircraft / Improvised bomber	1
De Havilland Dragon Rapide	Light aircraft / Improvised bomber	1
RWD-13	Light Aircraft	2
Beechcraft Bonanza B-35	Light Aircraft	2
Fairchild F-24R Argus	Light Aircraft	1
Taylorcraft Model C	Light Aircraft	2

Source: Adapted from Rubenstein and Goldman's book, Shield of David.

On May 27, 1948 the *Sherut Avir* formally transitioned to the Israeli Air Force or *Chel Ha'Avir* (חיל האוויר), as a part of the official establishment of the Israel Defense Forces (IDF). The available aircraft were not all very useful to the IAF in their primary design roles of light transport aircraft. Instead, the new IAF utilized the aircraft in other than designed ways. The light aircraft intended for recreational flight were used for the transport of small groups of soldiers or small pieces of cargo. Additionally, the light aircraft were utilized as forward observers for the ground forces, providing intelligence, surveillance, and reconnaissance for battlefield commanders. On May 25, 1948, two days prior to the IAF's establishment, the first military aircraft purchases began to arrive, and the first Douglas C-47 transport plane was made operational in Israel.[7]

The prevalent thought was that the war was won on the ground, and as such the battlefield commanders were the high-value assets for the defense of the country. The *Haganah*'s strategy and victory revolved around ground forces to hold back the enemy and maintain positive control of the new Israeli state. The IAF use was limited due to a lack of an explicit vision for Israeli airpower at the onset of the war for independence. This was mainly due to the existential threat that was coming from just across the borders from Egypt, Syria, and Jordan. This threat caused civilian and military commanders to focus on the defensive maneuvers of the ground forces and to subordinate the available airpower to them. Airpower reacted solely to the ground force commanders' needs.

---

[7] Rubenstein and Goldman, *Shield of David*, 22.

In this subordination to ground priorities, the IAF's roles consisted of aerial reconnaissance and improvised bombing, strictly in support of the ground commander. As the conflict continued and the Israelis acquired more airplane types, these roles expanded to include "air-to-air" combat, bombing, and something akin to a defensive counter air mission. However, in the beginning, the relevance and impact of the IAF lay in the imaginations of the airmen. They pushed the aircraft to their limits, conceived of innovative ways to compensate for lack of fighter and bomber aircraft, and demonstrated a high degree of dedication and work ethic to keep these high-value and low-density assets in the war.

The innovative mindset of the early Israeli airman cannot be undervalued. For example, in the absence of bombers, they fitted antiquated light aircraft with bomb racks out of necessity to create an aircraft capable of delivering munitions on the battlefield. When such modifications could not work, "bombardiers" were assigned to light aircraft to hurl grenades and homemade bombs out of the aircraft towards the enemy forces on the ground.[8] "Grenades and light machineguns constituted the Air Force's initial armament. But soon, Israeli-made, 20-50-kilogram bombs were put into service. The light craft thus was promoted to the rank of "bomber.""[9] The IAF's primary missions in 1948 were supply, reconnaissance, and bombardment and ground attack.

The first military plane that Israel acquired was a spoil of war. Israeli anti-aircraft fire struck an attacking Egyptian Spitfire which crash-landed on the beach near Herzliya, Israel. The pilot was captured, and Israeli aircraft maintenance personnel worked to make it operational again for the IAF. Once the IDF and its subordinate IAF were able to survive the initial Arab onslaught, the Israeli government obtained more aircraft, and the IAF could take to the skies against adversary forces. On June 4, the Israeli Fairchild aircraft was lost during a bombing raid against enemy ground forces. On May 29, 1948, the first four Israeli fighter aircraft, Czech Avia S-199 fighters, took to the skies for a combat mission, in a ground interdiction role, expanding the envelope of IAF capabilities from reconnaissance, "bombing," transport, and now air-to-air combat.[10] Still, these operations remained subordinate to ground support roles.

---

[8] Rubenstein and Goldman, 16–17.
[9] Yehuda; Hadar, Moshe; Ofer, ed., *Heyl Haavir Israel Air Force* (Tel Aviv, Israel: Pell Printing Words, Ltd, 1971), 29.
[10] Rubenstein and Goldman, 143.

Operation Yoav

After several months of defensive combat from May to September 1948, the IDF and specifically, the IAF was able to regroup sufficiently to launch the first Israeli offensive, named Operation *Yoav* (מבצע יואב). The operation took place in mid-October 1948 in an attempt to split the Egyptian forces in the south and open up the Negev desert for Israeli control. The IAF had acquired additional military grade aircraft with which to fight the Arabs (Table 2), expanding the types of mission and support they were able to provide to the IDF and nation. Operation *Yoav* opened with an aerial assault in which the IAF bombed and strafed aircraft stationed at the Egyptian Air Base at El Arish, marking the first Israeli offensive air operation.[11]

Table 2. IAF operational inventory on the eve of Operation Yoav.

Aircraft	Aircraft Type	Number of Aircraft
Boeing B-17G	Bomber	3
Douglas DC-3 Dakota	Transport	5
Bristol Beaufighter	Fighter	3
Lightplanes (Miscellaneous)	Light aircraft	40
Avia Messerschmitt S-199	Fighter	8
Supermarine Spitfire	Fighter	5
Curtiss C-46 Commando	Transport	6
Noorduyn Norsemen	Light aircraft	5

Source: Adapted from page 50 of Rubenstein and Goldman's book, Shield of David.

Despite these aircraft acquisitions, the Israeli Air Force was independent, and yet, no matter the capability that the aircraft presented, the IAF's potential was seconded to the needs of the IDF ground forces and their commanders. Thus, although there were specific efforts devoted to strategic attack, the preponderance of the missions focused on reconnaissance for the ground forces, interdiction, close air support, and troop transport.

By the end of Operation Yoav, the IAF and its 150 pilots had flown over 239 sorties, dropped 151 tons of bombs, and struck 21 targets, enabling the subsequent IDF control over two-dozen villages in the Negev desert and the surrounding countryside.[12] The

---

[11] Rubenstein and Goldman, 143.
[12] Rubenstein and Goldman, 50.

significance of this operational victory had strategic effects in the region. The expansion of Israeli control down to the city of Eilat created a physical barrier of Israeli control in between the Arab nations along the Red Sea, preventing a land corridor between Egypt and Jordan.[13]

Overall, the Israeli War for Independence consisted of iterations of similar goals versus similar opponents. The IDF attempted to gain territory where it could and staved off the assaults in other locations. All the while, the IAF provided mobility, eyes-in-the-sky, and kinetic effects when possible. The war lasted until the spring of 1949, through three separate periods of fighting, and two United Nations (UN)-imposed ceasefires. The extra 2,500 square miles of land which the IDF controlled outside of the initial borders of Israel was granted to the state by the UN in the final arbitration of the end of the war.[14] Israel was a state in relative peace for the first time since its establishment.

The Transition of the Interwar Period

After the war for independence, military and civilian leaders had time to think about the future of the IDF. In these discussions about the future of Israeli warfare, the IAF leaders found that they were fighting against ground-minded members who could not conceive of the broader implications of an air force. Instead, senior officials led by Prime Minister David Ben Gurion maintained that they only needed just enough of an air force to support the ground forces, for the ground forces were the heart of any war. Many leaders of the IAF failed to get civilian and IDF leaders to fully realize its potential. This frustrating situation led three consecutive heads of the IAF to resign in under three years. Additional implications of this miscategorization of the IAF led to stringent budgets and no acquisition strategy. Instead, the IAF's purchases were more coincidental and reliant on external opportunity rather than driven from internal vision and requirements. This led to the IAF's inventory of a "hodgepodge" of many types of aircraft, very few of which were modern or the most updated models.[15] The IAF was in a disheveled state after the war for independence.

---

[13] Ahron Bregman, *Israel's Wars*, *Israel's Wars*, 2016, 32, https://doi.org/10.4324/9781315646893.
[14] Bregman, 33.
[15] Rubenstein and Goldman, *Shield of David*, 67.

This disheveled state was aggravated by the exodus of qualified and experienced personnel from the IAF. The *Mahal* volunteers, Jews and Zionists from outside Israel who fought in the War for Independence, returned to their homes abroad once the war was over.[16] It was not until the mid-1950s that an IAF leader would have a significant and long-lasting effect on the force. David Ben Gurion in his role as the Defense Minister assigned Major General Dan Tolkovski as the commander-in-chief of the IAF in 1953.[17] "His was a fateful appointment. Perhaps more than any other single individual, Tolkovski, a veteran of the Second World War, molded the Israeli Defence Force/Air Force into the crack fighting army it is today [1978]."[18] Tolkovski's vision and determination molded every aspect of the IAF from the beat-up survivor of the war of independence, into a deliberately honed fighting force.

Tolkovski, a South African native and World War II British Royal Air Force veteran, understood inherently the needs of a highly efficient fighting force. While addressing the inventory requirements of the IAF, he also revolutionized how the IAF operated. Possessing a vision of a lean multi-purpose and efficient force, he instituted higher standards of crew performance. Understanding that the adversaries of Israel would always have the numerical advantage in aircraft, he emphasized the need for qualitative superiority through continuous, rigorous training. The pilots had to excel in every aspect of their jobs, and that also applied down to the lowest ranking aircraft mechanic on the ground. Everyone in the combat and support chain was trained and drilled until they were the epitome of efficiency.[19]

Major General Tolkovski implemented a policy that continues to influence IAF aircraft acquisition even today. He perceived Israel's geographic position--surrounded by potential enemies on all sides--to preclude the luxury of a strategic bomber force since he assessed that Close Air Support (CAS) and support of the ground forces would always be the IDF's first priority. Like the strategic bomber, therefore, a fighter designed purely for air superiority was an unaffordable luxury to the IAF. Accordingly, multi-purpose fighter-

---

[16] Hadar, Moshe; Ofer, *Heyl Haavir Israel Air Force*, 47.
[17] David Ben Gurion spent over 15 years double-hatted as both the Prime Minister as well as the Minister of Defense.
[18] Rubenstein and Goldman, *Shield of David*, 66.
[19] Rubenstein and Goldman, 68.

bombers became the targeted acquisition. In this decision, Tolkovski is credited with standardizing equipment and reducing the wide variety of aircraft and equipment in the IAF inventory by focusing acquisition efforts and deliberately purging the IAF inventory of air and ground equipment to only those that would support his envisioned fleet.[20] In doing so, he minimized the costs and requirements for maintenance of the fleet; fewer airplane types means more uniformity in support of operations training and logistics. Although this may have created gaps in capabilities between aircraft that were designed purely for one purpose, e.g., air-to-air combat versus an Israeli multi-role fighter, Tolkovski believed the quality of his airmen and pilots would overcome that gap.

Even so, Major General Tolkovski had a difficult time convincing Prime Minister/Defense Minister Ben-Gurion of the necessity to modernize the already aging air force. The challenge was overcoming Ben-Gurion's paradigm that each kibbutz or village was a fortress that relied primarily on ground troops for protection. Air power was simply an auxiliary to the ground, and they did not continue to invest in it because its current inventory sufficiently satisfied ground requirements.[21] External variables and Tolkovski's determination overcame the inertia of a ground-centric IDF. The primary fighter aircraft of the IAF during the 1950s was the de Havilland DH 98 Mosquito FB6, but when the Egyptian Air Force (EAF) purchased 120 MiG-15 jet fighters, among other military equipment from the Soviet Union, the IAF had the rationale to begin a crisis acquisition of more modern and capable fighters. This resulted in the purchases of the British Gloster Meteor F8 and the French multi-role Dassault Ouragan with all-weather targeting capabilities and represented the true beginning of Tolkovski's standardization effort.[22]

In Tolkovski's vision of the IAF, unlike modern great air powers, the IAF did not have room to pursue aircraft designed for particular mission sets. Each targeted acquisition had to establish parity on the battlefield with its opponents, or more ideally, surpass them. The same held for every airman of the IAF. They had to be the best in all they did; there was no room for mediocrity in the mission for the state's survival. It was thanks to

---

[20] Simon Dunstan, *The Six Day War 1967: Sinai* (Long Island City: Osprey Publishing, 2009), 17.
[21] Rubenstein and Goldman, *Shield of David*, 67.
[22] Dunstan, *The Six Day War 1967: Sinai*, 28; Rubenstein and Goldman, *Shield of David*, 62.

Tolkovski's efforts that the IAF was ready to take on the challenges of the next decade beginning with the Suez Canal Crisis.

On the eve of the 1956 Suez Canal Crisis, the standardization effort had not culminated, but through eight years of aircraft purchases, the IAF inventory looked different than it had been during the War of Independence. The IAF's aperture of possible mission sets expanded. Its fighter and bomber force consisted of the P-51 Mustang, Boeing B-17, de Havilland Mosquito, Supermarine Spitfire, Gloster Meteor, Dassault Mystere IV, and Dassault Ouragan and pushed the maximum ranges of direct support missions for ground forces without needing to refuel. This variety also meant that the IAF could set up layers of functionality over a limited battle area from CAS, interdiction, reconnaissance, and direct attack without needing to sacrifice a mission set. The transport and mobility fleet was also expanded to include the Douglas DC-5, Miles M.57 Aerovan, Curtiss C-46 Commando, Douglas DC-3/C-47 Dakota, and Nord 2501 Noratlas. Now planners did not have to choose between using a single aircraft as either a transport or as a bomber. Lastly, the acquisition of helicopters began with the Hiller UH-12 to supplement the fixed-wing aircraft inventory.[23] More importantly, compared to their Arab foes, the men and women of the IAF were more disciplined, better trained, and more efficient at their combat roles, and thus ready to take on the next challenge.

Operation Kadesh: The Suez Canal Crisis

The 1956 Suez Canal Crisis was an interesting point in Israel's history. Although Israel had become accustomed to facing threats and incursions from its Arab neighbors, the Suez Canal Crisis would be the first time that Israel would work as part of a quasi-coalition and in an expeditionary manner. In July 1956, Egyptian President Gamal Abdel Nasser declared the nationalization of the Suez Canal. This outraged several in the international community; high on that list was Israel, the United Kingdom, and France. As such, the three countries developed a joint strategy to restore international control over the canal from the Egyptians. The plan consisted of an initial surprise attack by Israel under the name Operation *Kadesh* (קדש), followed by the introduction of a British and French force that would then act as a buffer between the Israelis and Egyptians. This would also place the Anglo-French force in physical control of the canal. The success of the operations

---
[23] Rubenstein and Goldman, *Shield of David*, 68.

(Operation *Kadesh* and the British-French Operation Musketeer) was contingent on the successful execution of a deception campaign leading up to the invasion.

The British and French deception plan was relatively straightforward. It aimed at convincing the Egyptians that the military rhetoric coming out of their respective countries was a bluff, while conditioning the Egyptians to routine foreign troop presence on Malta. On the other hand, the Israeli deception campaign was more complicated. The Israelis mobilized under cover of a border conflict with Jordan and used trainer aircraft spoofing the Identify-Friend-or-Foe signals of fighter patrols. Additionally, the IAF had also conditioned the Egyptian Air Force (EAF) by flying the same routes on daily morning training flights. These would be the same routes that Operation *Moked* would later follow in the opening acts of the Six Day War in 1967.[24]

Operation *Kadesh* was a success both tactically and strategically. Via its deception campaign, the IAF was able to catch the EAF off-guard. The IAF bombers and fighters launched at dawn that morning against the EAF airfields. Over the first few days of the conflict, the IAF was able to destroy approximately 80% of the EAF inventory, most of which were destroyed on the ground.[25] This allowed the British and French air forces to operate in the northern Suez Canal area relatively unimpeded. Additionally, it allowed the IDF armored units to advance forward and gain control of much of the Sinai Peninsula.

The 1956 Sinai campaign was a proving ground for IAF efficiency and professionalism, bringing airpower to the foreground of military planning. After the Sinai campaign, the "apparent supremacy of the tank and the airplane" became the core of doctrine as the IAF demonstrated efficacy in a variety of mission sets, to include a belief in the attainment of air superiority. This resulted in a major expansion and modernization of the IAF and additional introspection on posturing the force for the next fight.[26]

After the Sinai campaign, the IDF leadership analyzed the campaign to posture the IDF for the next war. From this self-critical analysis they derived seven focus areas for improvement of which the IAF drew upon four key lessons: Israel must never plan for

---

[24] B L Bluestone and J P Peak, "Air Superiority and Airfield Attack - Lessons From History" (McLean, VA, 1984), 130.
[25] Bluestone and Peak, 111.
[26] David Rodman, *Sword and Shield of Zion : The Israel Air Force in the Arab-Israeli Conflict, 1948-2012* (Portland, OR: Sussex Academic Press, 2013), 17.

international support in a military conflict; Israel must plan and prepare to fight with only what is in the country at the time of the conflict, requiring a strategic reserve of materiel; the IAF's roles of ground support and air superiority require an all fighter air force; the logistics operations of the IDF had to support rapid movements; command and control of the IDF had to facilitate command of both air and ground forces.[27] These elements were the critical inputs for the IDF and IAF planning processes for future contingencies against any potential adversaries.

The Six-Day War and Operation Moked

Never has the IDF been more ready and more prepared for war.
-Major General Yitzhak Rabin

The planning for Operation *Moked* began years before the actual start of the war. Derived from lessons and doctrine of the IAF era led by Major General Tolkovski, the IAF was ready for a critical preemptive strike against its adversaries. One of the tenets of Tolkovski's philosophy of Israeli air power was that the first objective in any future war would be to destroy the enemy's air force. Only then could the air force safely turn its attention to strike and reconnaissance missions supporting the ground forces.[28] After it experimented with such a successful raid on the EAF airfields as part of Operation *Kadesh*, the Israeli leadership was inspired by the value of airpower to any given military campaign. Operation *Moked* was modeled on Operation Barbarossa from World War II, with mission aims of destroying the enemy air forces on the ground before they could even take off.[29] The military campaign consisted of four ground-centric phases, all of which were predicated on the successful preemptive strike by the IAF of the EAF and the subsequent attainment of air supremacy.[30]

In the initial planning stages of Operation *Moked*, IDF senior leaders were unsure of who specifically the enemy might be in a future war. As such, four variations or branch plans of Operation *Moked* were established. In Operation *Moked* A, the attack would be

---

[27] Rita A. Springer, "Operation *Moked* and the Principles of War" (Naval War College, 1997), 4; Thomas E Griess, Roy K Flint, and United States Military Academy. Dept. of History., "Atlas of the Arab-Israeli Wars, the Chinese Civil War, and the Korean War," *The West Point Military History Series*, 1986, 9, https://doi.org/10.1109/TRO.2007.904911.
[28] Rubenstein and Goldman, *Shield of David*, 68.
[29] Eliezer Cohen, *Israel's Best Defense* (New York: Orion Books, 1993).
[30] Dunstan, *The Six Day War 1967: Sinai*, 16.

conducted strictly against Egypt. In Operation *Moked* B, only Syria would be attacked. Operation *Moked* C had two internal variants that the IAF would be facing both Egypt and Syria, or Egypt, Syria, and Jordan. Operation *Moked* D tasked the IAF for a fight against Egypt, Iraq, Jordan, Lebanon, and Syria.[31]

Egyptian actions in 1960 prompted a foreshadow of the Six Day War. In February 1960, Egypt deployed its forces to its border with Israel. The IAF responded quickly with a high degree of readiness demonstrating its effectiveness as a deterrent to "surprise" threats that the slower ground forces could not deter. Throughout the 1960s, the Soviet Union considered Egypt and Syria its Cold War proxies and supplied them with aircraft, tanks, heavy artillery, SAMs, and logistical support, skewing the power balance in the Arab states' favor. "This forever changed the geostrategic balance in the Middle East and shaped the IAF's dominant role in Israel's strategy for the Six Days War."[32]

President Nasser's aggressive rhetoric also continued through the 1960s, creating persistent anxiety in Israel towards an impending attack. On July 11, 1965, he stated, "the final account with Israel will be made within five years if we are patient. The Moslems waited 70 years until they expelled the Crusaders from Palestine."[33] The sentiment in Israel was that an invasion was inevitable. Thus, the Israeli intelligence apparatus focused on indications and warning of an impending Egyptian attack.

In 1967, Israeli intelligence was looking at Egyptian forces in Yemen, believing that Nasser would surely bring back his elite units that were engaged in a fight there before attacking Israel. Meanwhile, the political and sometimes physical fight with Syria over waterways, Palestinian paramilitary groups, and the control of demilitarized zones continued.[34] Israeli leaders could see potential sparks everywhere that could light the powder kegs that surrounded the country. Ironically, it was an unexpected Soviet intelligence report that would initiate the events of the Six Day War.

Soviet authorities provided both Syrian and Egyptian leaders with an intelligence report that Israel had amassed ten brigades on the border with Syria. In response to this

---

[31] Dunstan, 38.
[32] Shmuel L. Gordon, "Air Superiority in the Arab Israeli Wars, 1967-1982," in *A History of Air Warfare* (Dulles, VA: Potomac Books, 2010), 129–31.
[33] Bregman, *Isr. Wars*, 63.
[34] Bregman, 66.

message, Nasser mobilized his ground forces in support of a fellow Arab state. He intended to help deter and possibly defeat the Israeli threat mounting on Syria's borders. Unfortunately, the report had been inaccurate, and instead, the Egyptian actions projected the threat of invasion which the Israelis took seriously.[35] This series of misperceptions and inaccurate information led the Israeli leadership to dust off Operation *Moked* and prepare for an attack.

The IAF was severely outnumbered and outgunned by the combined forces of the Syrian, Jordanian, and Egyptian air forces. In June 1967, the IAF had approximately two hundred combat aircraft working out of four airfields, whereas the combined enemy forces had over 650 combat aircraft operating out of 35 airfields. As the main threat, the EAF accounted for nearly five hundred of those aircraft and 23 airfields.[36]

Table 3. IAF operational inventory on the eve of Operation Moked, 1 June 1967.

Aircraft	Aircraft Type	Number of Aircraft
Sud Vautour	Combat / Fighter	25
Dassault Mirage III CJ	Combat / Fighter	72
Dassault Super Mystere	Combat / Fighter	20-24
Dassault Mystere IV	Combat / Fighter	60
Dassault Ouragan	Combat / Fighter	40
Fouga Magisters	Combat / Fighter	76
Nord Noratlas	Transport	20-25
C-47	Transport	10
Boeing Stratocruiser	Transport	5-6
S-58	Helicopter	12
Alouette III	Helicopter	15
Super Frelon	Helicopter	6-12
Alouette II	Helicopter	2-6
S-55	Helicopter	2-3

Source: Adapted from Le Moniteur de l'Aeronautique 1966-67, in Rodney S. Crist, "Air Superiority: A Case Study" and page 96 of Rubenstein and Goldman's book, Shield of David.

---

[35] Bregman, 70.
[36] Bluestone and Peak, "Air Superiority and Airfield Attack - Lessons From History," 122–24.

Taking lessons learned from earlier deception operations, Israel combined previous deception tactics with new ideas to again gain the element of surprise over its adversaries. This time, the deception included publicizing the leave plans of thousands of Israeli soldiers that weekend, deceptive public statements by defense officials, and the IAF created a diversion to draw attention towards a blockaded port, causing the EAF to redeploy units. Additionally, the IAF adjusted the time of the attack to a later point in the day, which threw off the Egyptians who had expected that any attack would only occur at sunrise. Thus, the EAF's morning patrols had already returned to base when the Israeli offensive kicked off.[37]

The deception was effective, and the IAF had the opportunity to deal a fatal blow to the country's adversaries. As planned, the air phase called for a preemptive attack against EAF airfields and radar sites. The IAF specifically targeted runways to prevent take-offs and landings, hostile fighter and bomber aircraft to reduce the enemy's offensive and defensive capabilities, surface-to-air missile systems, and, lastly, radars to reduce the EAF's situational awareness of the battlespace. The targets were prioritized and attacked in a sequence based on their ability to facilitate an attack on the Israeli homeland.

In order to successfully accomplish this, the IAF understood that their small air force would have to complete many sorties in order to create the desired effect on the battlefield. Thankfully, the preparation, practice, and procedures ingrained in the IAF from Major General Tolkovski's era had worked to make the IAF a lean and efficient fighting machine. Everything about Operation *Moked* was timed to the minute. Aircraft maintenance crews stood ready to turn an aircraft around in under ten minutes, in order to gain precious minutes of air operations in each wave.[38] The IAF also leveraged a communications system that was established to deliver a warning of incoming problems with returning aircraft and ensure the crews were postured to fix everything in as little time as possible.[39] Additionally, fresh pilots stood by to take the next plane that landed up in the air for their mission. For every one aircraft, there were three pilots assigned and ready to fly it.[40]

---

[37] Jeremy Bowen, *Six Days* (New York: St. Martin's Press, 2005), 103.
[38] Rubenstein and Goldman, *Shield of David*, 68.
[39] Cohen, *Israel's Best Defense*, 195.
[40] Dunstan, *The Six Day War 1967: Sinai*, 30.

The hard work paid off for the IAF as the first day of Operation *Moked* was a resounding success. The first three hours were dedicated to disarming the EAF, and the subsequent three hours made quick work of the Jordanian and Syrian Air Forces. The preemptive strike had destroyed or grounded nearly all the adversary aircraft within six hours of the start of the operation. By the end of the first day, the IAF struck seventeen airfields and destroyed over 416 Arab aircraft; almost 80 of these were shot down in air-to-air combat.[41] The IAF was free to support the ground forces for the remainder of the war, but it was evident that the preparation for this conflict would go down in history. As Egyptian Brigadier General Tahsin Zaki stated, "Israel spent years preparing for this war whereas we prepared for parades."[42] Operation *Moked*'s successful planning, deception, and execution place it on the winner's podium of air battles in history.

Summary

At its inception, the IAF was a defensive force struggling for its survival alongside its sister services in the war of independence. After the war, the entire Israeli government, including the IDF, underwent a storming phase until it arrived at a set of norms that guided planning and operations. During this period of relative peace following the war of independence, the IAF was able to establish itself and prepare for the Sinai Campaign and Six Day War through a series of internal revolutionary changes, planning efforts, and aircraft acquisition plans. With a high level of preparedness and confidence, the IAF was able to prove the advantage an elite fighting force could provide to the overall state of national defense in both defensive and offensive operations. Though it established its credibility, it would still be subordinated to the IDF's overall ground campaign for the foreseeable future, possibly limiting the extent of the effect it could have in future campaigns.

---

[41] Dunstan, 39; Rubenstein and Goldman, *Shield of David*, 98. 39.
[42] Dunstan, *The Six Day War 1967: Sinai*, 39.

Chapter 3

David's Sky, 1967-1973

The Air Force with its great striking power has carried its fire beyond our horizons and sped swiftly from one front to another. Its strength has made it the defender at our gates and the mainstay of our safety.

Moshe Dayan
Israeli Minister of Defense

Introduction

The period covering 1967-1973 includes the War of Attrition and the Yom Kippur War. This chapter explores the impact of the Six-Day War on the IAF as the nation transitioned from that brilliant victory into the grueling War of Attrition with its Arab neighbors. This period culminates in the starkly contrasting operational losses of the Yom Kippur War to the astounding victory of 1967, the Operation Moked campaign. Finally, this chapter will explore the implications of this period in the history of Israeli Defense Forces (IDF) and the Israeli Air Force (IAF) as they faced a future characterized by a rapidly changing strategic landscape across the region.

The Aftermath of the Six-Day War

The Six-Day War was a significant victory for the IDF in its primary mission of defending the nation and ensuring its continued survival. Though the Israeli propaganda machine focused on images of paratroopers breaking through the Arab front lines in Jerusalem's Old City to secure the Kotel, or Western Wall, of the Temple Mount, the IAF was the true hero of the war. In the IAF's execution of Operation *Moked*, it gained air supremacy over the battlespace by destroying the Egyptian, Syrian, and Jordanian air forces while they were still largely on the ground. In doing so, the IAF guaranteed air supremacy and could provide overwhelming air support to IDF ground forces who pushed forward into enemy territory. Despite this massive achievement, the IAF's victory was not without loss, the force losing up to 20% in some of its aircraft inventory categories, as depicted in Table 4 below. In achieving victory, the IAF was left smaller and weaker.[1]

---

[1] Shmuel L. Gordon, "Air Superiority in the Arab Israeli Wars, 1967-1982," in *A History of Air Warfare* (Dulles, VA: Potomac Books, 2010), 136.

Table 4. IAF operational inventory for the month of June 1967.

Aircraft	Aircraft Type	Number of Aircraft June 1, 1967	Number of Aircraft June 30, 1967
Dassault Ouragons	Fighter-bombers	40	37
Dassault Mystere IV	Fighter-bombers	60	52
Dassault Super-Mystere	Fighter-bombers	24	21
Dassault Mirage III CJ	Interceptors	72	66
Sud Vautour II	attack aircraft	25	20
Fouga Magister	Fighter-bombers	76	70
Nord Noratlas	Transport	20-25	19
Boeing Stratocruiser	Transport	5-6	5
Douglas C-37	Transport	10	10
Super Frelon	Helicopter	6-12	6
Sikorsky S-55	Helicopter	2-3	2
Sikorsky S-58	Helicopter	12	12
Alouette II	Helicopter	2-6	2
Alouette III	Helicopter	15	Unk

Source: Adapted from pulled from Le Moniteur de l'Aeronautique 1966-67, in Rodney S. Crist, "Air Superiority: A Case Study" and page 96 of Rubenstein and Goldman's book, Shield of David.

The new status quo of a post-Six-Day War was problematic for Israel. Although Israel had acquired new land that increased its strategic depth, the IDF was not manned sufficiently to protect and preserve the newly acquired territories of the Sinai, West Bank and Golan. Additionally, the IDF was not designed for the long term, sustainment operations to do so.[2] What is more, it wasn't quite a time of peace for Israel, either.

Each side viewed the "end" of the Six-Day War differently. The Egyptians referred to it as Al-Naksa, or the Setback, rather than the end of a war. To them, those six days were the beginning of a continual conflict with Israel that would last until a cease-fire was called

---
[2] Murray Rubenstein and Richard Goldman, *Shield of David* (Englewood-Cliffs, New Jersey: Prentice-Hall, 1978), 104.

in 1970. Al-Naksa stretched until and transformed into the War of Attrition as a continuation of the struggle against Israel.[3]

Politically, the Six-Day War had some interesting effects on the global balance of power. From the time of Israel's independence, the USSR had been forging relations with both Israel and the surrounding Arab states as it groomed potential allies in the Cold War struggle against the US and Western democracies. However, it was not until the Israeli victories that led the Arab states to request even more Soviet support that the scale tipped more heavily to the Arab states. In contrast, the Western democracies filled that resultant gap in support to Israel, both politically and with military resources. Throughout the first two decades of Israel's independence, the US was still on the fence when it came to picking a side in the contentious Middle East conflict. The US saw itself as a mediator and did not want to show any favoritism that could undermine the peace efforts that it was trying to launch the region in the absence of formal peace talks after the Lausanne Conference of 1949.

Egyptian President Gamel Abdel Nasser's "Big Lie" during the Six-Day War pushed the US off the fence and onto the Israeli side. The "Big Lie," or more appropriately, Nasser's misinformation campaign during the Six-Day War, was his attempt to pull the Soviets into the fight by stating that the IAF was augmented by the US and British air forces.[4] His evidence came from the amount of destruction suffered by the Egyptian air force and high numbers of sorties flown by the IAF. As mentioned earlier, Israeli turn time between sorties was down to minutes, whereas the Egyptian Air Force was still counting turnarounds in hours. Thus, the math did not add up: how could such a small force conduct so many strikes if they operated in the same manner as the Egyptians. Thus, it was inconceivable to Nasser that the IAF won in the air on their own. Inadvertently, the "Big Lie" increased Soviet support for Egypt and cemented US support for Israel and its distancing from Cairo. Having picked a side—a friendly democracy in the Middle East—the US began selling aircraft and other weapons to Israel, and hoped to offset the Soviet influence in the region.[5]

---

[3] Simon Dunstan, *The Six Day War 1967: Sinai* (Long Island City: Osprey Publishing, 2009), 90.
[4] Dunstan, 89.
[5] Dunstan, 90.

Parallel expansions of the armed forces of both the Israelis and the Egyptians was another outcome of the Six-Day War. Coming quickly after the IAF's initial expansion just before the 1956 Sinai Campaign, the IAF underwent another round of growth after the Six-Day War. During this period, the IAF transitioned from a reliance on French to American aircraft. The US offered airplanes, helicopters, munitions, radars, and support equipment.[6] Following these purchases, the IAF became the most capable and well-funded arm of the IDF.[7]

The IAF's technological expansion was accompanied by doctrinal changes based on the changing conditions of the war in the air. The IDF's victory in the war vindicated its focus on the combined effects of armor and airpower. Thus, the victory reaffirmed the doctrine seeking air supremacy, at the outset of conflict ideally in a preemptive strike, and then quickly subordinating the IAF to support the ground forces, while the army employed armor as the tip of the spear to achieve objectives.[8] But, given the upgrading and hardening of the Integrated Air Defense Systems (IADS) of both Egypt and Syria, in the wake of the IAF's victory and despite its upgrades to its aircraft, the IAF would most likely no longer be able to destroy an adversary air force on the ground at the kickoff of a war. Instead, the IAF's planners saw the priority challenge of future conflicts as the destruction or disabling of those IADS in order to facilitate air superiority and freedom of maneuver.[9]

The War of Attrition Begins

The War of Attrition is often categorized as one of the proxy wars that occurred during the Cold War between the US and the USSR. As discussed, the US and USSR had increased their military, political, and economic support to the fighters in their respective corners.[10] Although the direct participation of these great powers in this war was not as obvious as in others such as Korea and Vietnam, the great power influence is still evident. If it had not been for the resupplying of the Arab states by the Soviet Union, they would not have been in a solid position to pursue action against Israel after the defeat of the Six Day War.

---

[6] Gordon, "Air Superiority in the Arab Israeli Wars, 1967-1982," 136.
[7] David Rodman, *Sword and Shield of Zion : The Israel Air Force in the Arab-Israeli Conflict, 1948-2012* (Portland, OR: Sussex Academic Press, 2013), 18.
[8] Rodman, *Sword and Shield of Zion : The Israel Air Force in the Arab-Israeli Conflict, 1948-2012.*
[9] Rodman, 18.
[10] Gordon, "Air Superiority in the Arab Israeli Wars, 1967-1982," 136.

The period immediately following the Six Day War until the "formal" declaration of war housed many clashes between the Egyptian and Israeli militaries. The first clash occurred in October 1967, when an Egyptian ship torpedoed and sunk an Israeli military ship in the international waters off Port Said. Another major conflict occurred in September 1968, when Israel and Egypt exchanged artillery barrages across the Suez Canal, inflicting heavy casualties on both sides. The IAF conducted strikes against operational targets like bridges, and delivered ground troops for raids into Egypt.[11] After this period of clashes, came a measure of quiet that lasted from November 1968 until March 1969. During the two years following the Six Day War, the IDF constructed the fortified Bar Lev line, a 180-kilometer line of thirty-two fortifications or strongpoints, ranging from Ras el-Aish to Port Tawfik. A second "line" was built east of the first, consisting of eleven additional fortifications to provide a measure of depth. Once constructed, this line became the focus of the artillery barrages from Egypt.[12]

Egypt formally began what President Nasser called the War of Attrition in April 1969.[13] Politically, it only began once the Soviet Union agreed with President Nasser's proposed goals and strategy. Egypt's strategy during the War of Attrition focused on inflicting human casualties. The goal was to kill as many Israeli soldiers as possible while gaining needed operational expertise, and maintaining an ongoing air battle with the IAF.[14] Thus, the "war" opened with a "ceaseless" barrage of artillery along the Israeli occupied eastern bank of the Suez Canal. The Egyptians had strategically placed new Soviet-made SA-2 surface-to-air missile (SAM) systems near their artillery batteries to protect them from IAF attack. Soon after, terrorist organizations from Syria and Palestine, now located in Jordan would join the battle against Israel.

The aerial portion of the War of Attrition formally began on July 20. 1969.[15] The first IAF targets were Egyptian artillery batteries and posts along the Suez Canal. Its first mission was to acquire freedom of maneuver over the canal to enable the actions of ground

---

[11] Ahron Bregman, *Israel's Wars, Israel's Wars*, 2016, 99, https://doi.org/10.4324/9781315646893.
[12] Bregman, 101.
[13] Aharon Lapidot, ed., *Open Skies* שמיים נקיים: *The Israeli Air Force: 40 Years* (Tel Aviv, Israel: Israeli Ministry of Defense and Peli Press, 1998), 123.
[14] Gordon, "Air Superiority in the Arab Israeli Wars, 1967-1982," 136–37.
[15] Gordon, 137.

forces.[16] The IDF had no effective response to the Egyptian artillery, and faced with growing casualties, leveraged the IAF as flying artillery. Additionally, the IAF was quickly integrating newly acquired "U.S.-made Skyhawks, Phantoms, CH-53 cargo helicopters, missiles, radars, and various other weapons systems into its operational force."[17] The IAF's new Skyhawk aircraft, arriving in December 1967, replenished the losses of the IAF's other fighter-bombers and were used as a workhorse during the War of Attrition, accounting for a large number of bombing missions and air-to-ground tactical sorties.[18] It would be months before the IAF attained a sufficient degree of air superiority, enough to allow the IAF to attack adversary ground forces in Close Air Support (CAS), interdiction, and ground attack roles.[19]

The first IAF offensive was called Operation Boxer. It was a bombing campaign of Egyptian military positions, air defense units, and artillery along the Suez Canal. Although it was tactically effective and the IAF destroyed equipment and periodically degraded Egyptian functions along the canal, it did not achieve the strategic effect of stopping the casualties and bloodshed of the static military positions firing upon one another. Additionally, in conducting Operation Boxer, the IAF consistently placed itself within the range of the Egyptian SAM systems, suffering increasing IAF losses.[20]

A Turning Point: Operation Priha

Once the IAF had earned its breathing room with blood and sweat, its leaders could conceive of taking an offensive posture. Their first attempt was Operation *Priha*, a plan designed for deep operations in enemy territory with the goal of forcing President Nasser's resignation.[21] Operation *Priha* had over twenty parts, each consisting of a deliberately planned strike and show of force and was conducted over the course of January to April 1970. As part of Operation *Priha*, the IAF targeted the Egyptian IADS, ground units, resupply and other military enabling targets. It destroyed most of the SAM sites surrounding Cairo and shot down Egyptian MiG fighters over the target area. With these actions, the IAF achieved local air superiority over the Nile Delta. Concurrently, the IAF

---

[16] Lapidot, *Open Skies* שמיים נקיים: *The Israeli Air Force: 40 Years*, 137.
[17] Lapidot, 137.
[18] Lapidot, 132.
[19] Lapidot, 137.
[20] Bregman, *Isr. Wars*, 103.
[21] Gordon, "Air Superiority in the Arab Israeli Wars, 1967-1982," 137.

conducted a show of force by sending a pair of F-4 Phantom aircraft to Damascus to let loose a sonic boom as a warning that the city was not untouchable.[22] The limited success of the operation left Israeli Prime Minister Golda Meir dissatisfied; she had hoped that the shock of exposing the vulnerabilities of the Egyptian leadership, military units, and civilians would cause the subsequent resignation of the Egyptian President. Instead, Operation *Priha* led to entirely unexpected results and implications over the battlespace.[23]

As a result of Operation *Priha*, Egypt requested additional help from Moscow, which arrived in the form of an advanced IADS. The Soviet support was manifested in equipment, training, and support personnel to guide Egyptian operations. The IADS proved fatal to the IAF pilots. The SAM systems were dangerous enough to interfere with IAF operations, deterring and defeating then by threatening the scarce aircraft that Israel had available. Also, most of Israel's aircraft were not capable enough to outmaneuver or outsmart the SAM systems. However, the purchase of the Phantom F-4 aircraft from the US provided Israel with a plane that could more safely conduct operations within those SAM engagement rings and survive, though it too was not invincible.

Soon, the Egyptians and Soviets noted the increase in survival rates of Israeli aircraft flying in the Egyptian SAM rings. Soviet support increased, and their pilots took to the air, patrolling their "on-loan" air defense system and threatening the IAF's ability to extend the air superiority envelope via air combat. The IAF and Soviet pilots engaged in a single definitive air battle in which the Soviets suffered heavy losses, leading both to avoid engagement with one another. Additionally, the Soviet-made surface to air missile systems were moved towards the Suez Canal, extending a blanket of protection over the "Egyptian-side" and inflicted losses on the small IAF as it tried to limit the eastward movement of those systems. The IAF had no technological or operational solutions to overcoming the newly enhanced Egyptian IADS. The Soviet interference affected air objectives, forcing the Israeli government to limit the IAF's role to "retaining air superiority over the canal and about thirty kilometers westward to defend ground forces deployed along the east bank of the Suez Canal."[24]

---

[22] "The Israeli Air Force: 1970s Events Log," accessed April 3, 2019, http://www.iaf.org.il/837-7128-en/IAF.aspx.
[23] Gordon, "Air Superiority in the Arab Israeli Wars, 1967-1982," 137.
[24] Gordon, 138–39.

In response to the Soviet-Israeli air engagement and increased US support to Israel in the engagement, the USSR encouraged President Nasser to accept a ceasefire for fear of exacerbating the situation further. Thus, after over a year of the war, Israel and Egypt signed a cease-fire on 7-8 August 1970. Over the course of approximately 385 days of a brutal aerial war, the IAF conducted approximately 12,500 sorties, of which 10,500 were against Egypt.[25] Though Israel may consider the war a victory, or at the least not a loss, there were many lessons to learn.

The introduction of newer Soviet military technology upset the balance for which the IAF and IDF leaders had planned. Though the quality and training of the IDF were still higher than that of the Egyptians, there does come the point in which strategy cannot outperform technology and a balance of both effective strategy and modern technology is needed to be successful in the battlespace. The existing IAF inventory could not overcome the threats posed by the Soviet SAM missile systems, and it prevented the required air superiority that would have enabled extensive ground operations. Additionally, the IAF's leaders maintained the strategies and tactics of the 1967 war, as they pressed forward in their planning, thus missing the global transformation of war from an older, World War II-style battle to a more modern war shaped by advanced technologies.[26] That being said, the IAF's air-to-air engagement statistics improved from the 1967 war to through War of Attrition, showing that the continued focus on high-quality personnel and training proved effective in the IAF construct for this purpose.

The War of Attrition ended with neither side gaining or losing territory. The attribute of "attrition" describes the casualty and losses of the ground forces and civilians in the war. By contrast, the IAF suffered relatively few aircraft losses, but even two dozen losses of its most advanced fighters were a significant hit to its inventory and capabilities. The IAF attempted to replenish its ranks with foreign aircraft, but was still encountering difficulty. Though some progress could be made in that area, it was more difficult to replenish the experience of those that had been lost during the war. While some lessons were learned from this long year of fighting, the IAF still had not fully realized the

---

[25] Gordon, 139.
[26] Robin D. S Higham and Stephen John Harris, *Why Air Force Fail: The Anatomy of Defeat* (Lexington, KY: University Press of Kentucky, 2006), 80.

cascading effects that advanced systems with guided missiles could have on their future plans and operations.[27] Additionally, the IDF had not fully grasped the implications and extent of the Soviet support for the Arab militaries. Lastly, the IDF primarily used the IAF in ground support, "flying artillery," and interdiction roles. The only strikes outside those target sets would be to enable achieving air superiority. These would be critical errors in the upcoming war.

The Yom Kippur War

After the successful campaigns in earlier Arab-Israeli wars, the IAF became guilty of the particular hubris that is born solely of great victory. As it continued to be carried aloft in the winds of its successes, the IAF postured for war in the ways it always had, consequently preparing itself for the wrong war, i.e. the last one.[28] In the summer after the War of Attrition, the IAF introduced airborne defensive measures to outmaneuver and survive the Soviet SA-2 and SA-3 surface to air missile systems that they had encountered around the Suez Canal in Egypt. These two systems had been the top-of-the-line SAM exports of the Soviet Union. Together, they created point defense and area defense rings that could reach medium- and high-altitude targets flying at high speeds. Their associated radars could provide early warning as far out as seventy miles. The IAF learned and trained to overcome these threats.

However, the Israelis failed to account for the massive Egyptian IADS buildup, and its subsequent capabilities. Though much Israeli research and work had been done in electronic countermeasures and the Israeli technologies industry was ramping up to support these efforts, they had yet to figure out how to outmaneuver or jam a SA-6, which, unfortunately would be the advanced surface to air missile system provided by the Soviets to the Egyptian military in advance of the war.[29] Operationally and tactically, the SA-6 would force IAF aircraft to operate lower than planned, and into the fatal envelopes of the ZSU-23 anti-aircraft artillery guns and SA-7 MANPADS.[30] The ZSU-23 is a self-propelled radar-guided anti-aircraft gun, whose radar guidance increases its efficacy and accuracy.

---

[27] Rubenstein and Goldman, *Shield of David*, 110.
[28] Rubenstein and Goldman, 122; Ervin J. Kis, "Techniques of Gaining Israeli Air Superiority in the 1973 War, Better Known as ' The Yom Kippur War '" 7, no. 3 (2008): 407.
[29] Rubenstein and Goldman, *Shield of David*, 123.
[30] Rubenstein and Goldman, *Shield of David*.

The MANPADS, or man-portable air defense system, posed a greater threat. These are light, easily transportable, passive, infrared-guided systems that do not emit radar signals and thus, would not provide early warning to pilots as they approached. Their missiles quickly and silently approach an aircraft until it is too late.

After the bloodshed and drain of the long War of Attrition, the Israelis were weary of fighting. The ceasefire that ended the War of Attrition allowed the Israelis to regroup and recuperate after the extended battles. The nation had existed for 26 years and senior leaders were rotating out of the military service to act as government officials or live as pensioners. But, the reprieve was one-sided; while Israel caught its breath and remained confident in its abilities, Egypt and Syria were already planning the next attack against the young state.

The objectives of both Arab nations would be tempered in the coming Yom Kippur War compared to earlier Arab-Israeli wars. In the earlier wars, the objectives were the defeat of Israel and reclamation of the land for the Arabs, erasing the Zionist state altogether. In a sense, it was an absolute war. By comparison, the Yom Kippur War was a limited war. The Egyptian objectives for the Yom Kippur war were "to capture a thin strip of the eastern bank of the Suez Canal and to destroy the IDF's armored divisions by exploiting the advantage of air superiority over the canal," thereby meeting the new Egyptian president's, Anwar Sadat, limited strategic political goals.[31] In preparation for this, President Sadat's Air Vice-Marshal, Hosni Mubarak, was assigned as the principal planner for this attack on Israel. He pursued an equipment acquisition strategy to update the EAF's capabilities, as well as enter joint planning for operations with the Syrian and Libyan Air Forces (though Libya did not ultimately participate). He pushed training and aimed to increase the quality of the EAF pilots, recognizing the gaps in capabilities between the two militaries. Lastly, Mubarak was a strong advocate for President Nasser's limited strategic objectives, understanding that in foregoing the direct assault, it would increase the survivability of the Egyptian military in its war against Israel.[32] Additionally, the suspected presence of nuclear weapons in Israel acted as a deterrent and limiter for Egypt's political and military goals.

---

[31] Gordon, "Air Superiority in the Arab Israeli Wars, 1967-1982," 141.
[32] Higham and Harris, *Why Air Force Fail: The Anatomy of Defeat*, 82.

As Israel became more enmeshed in the quagmire that is international politics, it added layers of complexity to its once simple and straightforward mission of survival of the state. As the people of Israel sat in their synagogues throughout the country on the holiest day of the Jewish year, Yom Kippur (the Day of Atonement), praying to be sealed in the book of life, Israeli leaders were fighting their own internal battles. Although intelligence had pointed out the increasing chances of a war around October 6, 1973, this time the preemptive attack was not the unanimously accepted solution. There was still too much doubt as to whether the expected strike from Syria would be a single, limited event or an opening act to a full war. Despite this, IAF officials wanted to launch a preemptive strike, like the one that had worked in the Six Day War. This time, the civilians stopped the military from acting.[33]

For Prime Minister Golda Meir and Defense Minister Moshe Dayan, it was more important for Israel's grand strategy that it not be the first to strike.[34] Israel had worked diligently to garner international support and establish relationships, particularly across the African continent, and it did not want to damage the relationships with a perceived aggressive act. The gamble that the ministers took was great, and the payoff is still debated.

On October 6, 1973 the Egyptian and Syrian armies conducted their coordinated opening gambits, and struck at Israel, causing the IDF to scramble in response. But, after two years of relative peace, it took the panicked Israeli military to reduce the fog and friction of this new war through organized operations and discipline.[35] It was in this fog, that the Egyptian Air Force struck airfields in Israel, attempting to ground aircraft and destroy the IAF before it could have a chance to defend itself.

---

[33] Gordon, "Air Superiority in the Arab Israeli Wars, 1967-1982," 123; Bregman, *Isr. Wars*, 128.
[34] Eliezer Cohen, *Israel's Best Defense* (New York: Orion Books, 1993), 324.
[35] Cohen, 327.

Table 5. IAF operational inventory in October 1973.

Aircraft Type	Number of Aircraft October 6, 1973
Fighters and Multirole	390
Helicopters	70
Cargo Planes	46

Source: Adapted from Shmuel Gordon's essay "Air Superiority in the Arab Israeli Wars, 1967-1982" on page 142 of A History of Air Warfare.

The Arab air forces found the IAF unprepared to defend the nation against such a surprise attack. Complicating the delays that came from senior leaders' decisions, poor communication and understanding led the force to increased unpreparedness. Rather than the preemptive strike which had become the IDF's modus operandi to increase odds of survival and success, the IDF was completely in a reactionary mode. The IAF concentrated on defending the skies over Israel, staving off the onslaught of attacking ground forces, and supporting the ground commanders with close air support.[36]

President Sadat set limited military aims for Egypt's war with Israel to facilitate his grand strategy goals of "breaking the stalemate in the Arab-Israeli conflict and create conditions ultimately conducive to a settlement consistent with Egypt's interests."[37] His military strategists also crafted limited objectives to achieve the desired victory. Although the Arab militaries outnumbered the IDF, they avoided the temptation of mounting an all-out single consolidated strike. They knew this strike, though tempting, would play to the strengths of the IDF, and expose them to the typical strikes that enabled Israeli victory in the past. Instead, they planned to draw Israel into a two-front war, rather than be drawn into a war with her at a starting disadvantage. The Syrians planned to attrit the IDF forces on the Golan front, and the Egyptians were to do similarly in the Sinai Peninsula. Key to this plan would in drawing the IAF into established IADS sectors, crippling the IDF's air arm.[38]

---

[36] Gordon, "Air Superiority in the Arab Israeli Wars, 1967-1982," 143.
[37] James W Bean and Craig S Girard, "Anwar Al-Sadat's Grand Strategy in the Yom Kippur War," *National War College*, 2001, 1, http://www.dtic.mil/dtic/tr/fulltext/u2/a442407.pdf.
[38] Rubenstein and Goldman, *Shield of David*, 124.

The Israelis were completely reactionary in the beginning. In their haste, IDF senior leaders determined the Suez Canal as the most threatening attack, and ordered the IAF there first to overtake the Egyptian IADS.[39] As in previous wars, the IAF's primary goal immediately became gaining air superiority while also providing CAS to the IDF ground units.[40] The intelligence just was not there to highlight the flaws in that decision. This would not be an easy nor quickly achievable objective.

During the first few days of the war, the IAF responded in any way it could deter and defeat enemy attacks. In the absence of other means, IAF fighter aircraft were used to shoot down enemy transport helicopters. The incoming Egyptian helicopters were filled with ground forces aimed at attacking ground and air bases throughout the Negev in Israeli occupied Sinai. Although anti-aircraft artillery (AAA) defenses protected the bases, they could not range them along the routes and landing zones. As such, the fighter aircraft were dispatched against the defenseless helicopters, and successfully engaged them, saving bases from direct assaults.[41] In the event that the adversary aircraft were able to reach an IAF airfield, they conducted bombing and strafing runs. Fortunately, that put them within the engagement envelopes of the IDF's anti-aircraft-artillery, such as L-70 cannons.[42]

Israel tried to launch Operational Plan *Tagar* or Challenge, to affect the Egyptian system. As part of a broader series of iterations, Operational Plans *Tagar* 4 and 5 specifically focused solely on Egypt. In the former, the IAF would target missile sites first to achieve a decisive advantage immediately. In *Tagar* 5, which considered AAA as the most serious threat to the penetrating aircraft, IAF first went after the AAA and delayed attacking surface to air missile systems until till the second wave. Regardless of the selected plan, half of the sorties would be allocated to airfield strikes. This was a preemptive suppression of enemy air defenses campaign to enable the IAF's primary missions. Unfortunately, in the fog of war, the execution of Operational Plan *Tagar,* which was intended to merge parts of both plans omitted targeting of the surface to air missile systems.

---

[39] Gordon, "Air Superiority in the Arab Israeli Wars, 1967-1982," 144.
[40] Gordon, 144.
[41] Cohen, *Israel's Best Defense*, 340.
[42] Cohen, 348.

AAA and airfields were left marginally damaged, but the primary threat to aircraft remained untouched.[43]

Unlike the plans for which the IDF and IAF had drilled and prepared, this situation put them in very reactionary roles. Rather than follow the deliberately planned roles and steps that had been outlined for an offensive, the IDF was trying to survive the initial onslaught. But, when the adversary forces came in contact with IDF troops, all resources were redirected to support those troops in contact. IAF sorties were redirected to conduct air-to-air intercept missions instead of launch attacks in Syria and Egypt, changing the targets for Operation *Dugman*.[44]

Following on the heels of Operations *Tagar's* failures, Operation *Dugman* held promise, but was ill-planned, rushed, and poorly timed. The targets for which the pilots had prepared were changed at the last minute from Egyptian IADS to Syrian IADS. As the IAF Phantoms were being sent northeast to strike at Syrian missile systems, the pilots quickly realized their location intelligence on the targets was inaccurate.[45] Though the strike and all the combat resources had been pivoted from Egypt to Syria, the required Intelligence, Surveillance, and Reconnaissance efforts had not, and this undermined the efficacy of the entire operation.[46]

In another instance of reactionary operations and less deliberate planning, the IDF leaders and Israeli ministers were gravely concerned with fourteen bridges the Egyptians built across the canal, enabling the crossing of ground forces into the Sinai Peninsula. Thus, the IAF was tasked with destroying the bridges. Actual destruction of a bridge is difficult, and instead the functionality of the bridge is targeted by dropping spans of it. The problem came when the Egyptian ground forces lay ready to conduct emergency repairs on these bridges, bringing them back to operational status, sometimes in mere hours. This created a drain on IAF resources as they had to conduct restrike operations on these same bridges time and again.[47] These examples are demonstrative of the earlier efforts and mistakes born

---

[43] Gordon, "Air Superiority in the Arab Israeli Wars, 1967-1982," 145.
[44] Cohen, *Israel's Best Defense*, 348.
[45] Gordon, "Air Superiority in the Arab Israeli Wars, 1967-1982," 145.
[46] Gordon, 146.
[47] Cohen, *Israel's Best Defense*, 354.

of ill-chosen planning efforts and decisions. Despite these failures, the IAF was still able to capitalize on some lessons, technology, and its high-quality force.

Survival Techniques

As a method of saving the IAF's precious assets but maintaining its efficacy, the IAF launched denial and deception operations. The IAF lured Arab air defense units in opposite directions to increase the survivability of the IAF aircraft on mission. Other times it was conducted as a part distraction, part strike, as the groups attacked from the same direction.[48]

Events unfolded as Egypt's military leaders planned, and the IAF was lured into the IADS rings. Approximately fifty first-line combat aircraft were destroyed, half of whom were taken out by the SA-6s against which the IAF had not developed defensive measures.[49] This was devastating to the small yet elite force. Observing the initial Israeli losses sounded alarms for the US. American leaders understood that Israel was their foothold within the Middle East, and were loath to see it lose it to Soviet-backed Arab states. Thus, the Yom Kippur War began to change from a war whose outcome lay strictly in strategy and tactics, to one that relied on external support for both sides. The American resupply effort was crucial to enabling an Israeli counteroffensive and ceasefire. The US supplied the IDF and IAF with more modern weaponry and aircraft, including more Skyhawks, that helped sway the tide of war.[50] Additionally, the Israeli industry and necessity for operational innovation increased IDF and IAF options on the battlefield.

For instance, the IAF used Unmanned Aerial Vehicles (UAVs) in the absence of manned aircraft to execute certain missions. Initially, the UAVs were used as decoy targets to distract enemy forces from IAF manned aircraft conducting strike missions. Later in the fight against terrorism, they would be used for intelligence, surveillance, and reconnaissance purposes as the technology would advance. But, for the purposes of the Yom Kippur War, they were aimed at increasing the survivability of the few aircraft the IAF maintained.[51]

---

[48] Kis, "Techniques of Gaining Israeli Air Superiority in the 1973 War, Better Known as ' The Yom Kippur War ,'" 412.
[49] Rubenstein and Goldman, *Shield of David*, 125.
[50] Rubenstein and Goldman, 126.
[51] Kis, "Techniques of Gaining Israeli Air Superiority in the 1973 War, Better Known as ' The Yom Kippur War ,'" 413.

As the IAF expanded its helicopter inventory, it was able to send its precious fighter-bombers against targets in more highly contested areas. For other mission requests, the IAF deployed helicopters in troop carrier and ground attack roles. The ground attack role was enhanced by the innovative use of weaponry. The IAF mounted French-made AS-11 guided missiles and American TOW missiles on the attack helicopters. This enabled precision anti-tank strikes versus the enemy's armored columns and fortifications.[52]

Lastly, the IAF was saved by its developments and acquisition of electronic warfare technology. Electronic jamming was directed toward Arab IADS to increase the survivability of IAF aircraft and elongate the element of surprise for strikes, if only by a few seconds. Typically, the IAF radio jammers aimed to keep the jamming operational for the duration of an attack. Additionally, the IDF outfitted many types of units and vehicles with these capabilities. UAVs, ground-based jamming units, and even a specially modified Boeing 737 Stratocruiser became the blinders for attacks against enemy targets.[53]

Ultimately, after 16 days of war, a ceasefire was declared on October 22, 1973. Israel had survived the war by the skin of its teeth, barely coming out ahead. Many factors contributed to the devastating losses of those two weeks, creating compounding effects. First, was the national civilian leaders' insistence on absorbing the first blow to maintain good standing with the international community including other Muslim countries. Second were the internal errors contributing to incorrect timing on the attacks and operations on opening day. Lastly, the IDF's preparation for the next war was same as that for the last, ignoring the Arab advances in equipment and training driven by their losses at the hands of the Israelis in 1967. Though it was a difficult and painful time for the IDF, it provided an opportunity and impetus for the IAF to break its operational mold and demonstrate an ability to affect strategic targets.

Yom Kippur War Vignette: Air Raid on Syrian General Command

Amid the struggle and smoke of the Yom Kippur War, the Syrian government elected to augment the conventional war which it had undertook with a newer weapon. On the third day of the war, October 9, 1973, Syrian ground forces launched Soviet-made 9K52 Luna-M "Frog" surface-to-surface missiles, landing in Migdal HaEmek in Northern

---

[52] Kis, 414.
[53] Kis, 415–16.

Israel, close to the Syrian border.[54] In doing so, it had attacked population centers, specifically Israeli settlements. A second set of Frog missiles struck Ramat David air base, close to the center of the country. This became too much for the Israeli government, and a strike against Syria was ordered.[55]

The Israeli government was outraged by the Syrian Frog missile attack, and acted decisively to set an example that would be remembered by Israeli adversaries, present and future. The IAF launched a series of strikes to deliberately disrupt the Syrian war-making capacity, striking strategic and economic targets, specifically its command and control, oil industry, and electric power system. At the top of the list was the Syrian Central Command and the Syrian Air Force Headquarters in Damascus. The two buildings lay near one another at the heart of the Syrian capital city. These targets would be one of the deepest (strategic) strikes Israel would execute, at approximately 136 miles from the nearest air base.[56] The operation was intended to have strategic, moral, and psychological effects on the Syrians, specifically jarring the Syrian senior leaders and hopefully insert a pause into their operations and command and control.

Israel had been married to its armor-airpower doctrine that had proven itself in prior wars. Yet, when a need to strike a long-range target presented itself, the armor-airpower doctrine could not satisfy it. Instead, IDF leaders were fortunate to have become more air-minded over the previous 25 years of warfare, and saw in the IAF an opportunity and a tool. Suddenly, the opportunity to affect an entire adversary target system was within grasp. The attack against the Syrian headquarters was part of a plan to achieve a strategic goal. The intentions of this air raid were multilayered. In the first layer, this was a retaliatory act for the ballistic missile attack on Israel, against a target of perceived strategic physical and psychological effect. But, at a deeper level, Israel hoped to deter Jordan from joining the war and prove to its active enemies that despite the beatings it had received early in the war, it was still capable of bringing the fight to them.

---

[54] Rubenstein and Goldman, *Shield of David*, 127; Cohen, *Israel's Best Defense*, 344.
[55] Cohen, *Israel's Best Defense*, 357.
[56] Distance calculated from Ramat David air base in Northern Israel to the center of Damascus. Cohen, 357. Although previous strikes ranged near this distance as the IAF attacked targets in Cairo, this was the first set of targets with hopes of strategic effect.

The eight-ship formation of Phantoms were able to successfully strike their assigned targets. The top floors of the Central Command's building were destroyed and the Syrian Air Force headquarters was partially damaged. Due to the damage, but command centers were forced to transfer their responsibilities to other buildings, causing a break in their command and control as well as a psychological effect.[57]

Nuclear Deterrence and War Aims

The Yom Kippur War represented one of the last traditional force-on-force wars that Israel would participate in until present day. It also is one of the last major opportunities that its enemies had to strike a vulnerable country with relative freedom of action due to a low-alert military and deliberate Israeli political maneuvering. Yet, neither Egypt nor Syria chose to expand their limited objectives to strike at the heart of the country and its people. As indicated earlier, the coordinated attack focused on the IDF and IAF's capabilities and only in the Golan Heights and Sinai Peninsula. This made military sense as it limited the Israeli options and kept the Arab forces out of the envelope of IAF capabilities. But, another lesser acknowledged aspect of the limited war objectives must also be acknowledged. Years later, President Anwar Sadat of Egypt would also confess that both Syria and Egypt feared that if they pushed Israel too far that the government would have responded with a nuclear response.[58] It was believed that nuclear deterrence could create a lasting peace in a state-on-state setting, because the alternative to peace would be too terrible to risk.[59]

Summary

Although the IAF and IDF in 1973 had been surprised and confused strategically by the coordinated attack from Syria and Egypt, the IAF responded effectively and courageously at the tactical levels. Not only had the IAF helped to ensure the survival of Israel, but it was also able to launch counteroffensives into both Syria and Egypt while also deterring Jordan from joining in the fray. Additionally, this caused the USSR to push its Arab clients for a peace settlement while US diplomats also engaged in shuttle diplomacy between both sides.

---

[57] Cohen, 359.
[58] Shimon Peres, *No Room for Small Dreams: Courage, Imagination and the Making of Modern Israel* (UK: Hachette, 2017), 104.
[59] Peres, 104.

Tolkovski's legacy of quality, efficiency, and training continued to have a great effect on the IAF, even fifteen years later. It was the quality of the IAF's personnel that reduced the effects of the enemies' numerical superiority. But, the IAF's numerical inferiority made every loss hurt all the more. These losses spurred another round of introspection and planning for future conflicts. After the Yom Kippur War, the armor-airpower doctrine transitioned to a more balanced and combined arms approach spurring advanced aircraft acquisition, increased exploration of electronic warfare systems, and UAVs.[60]

The culmination of the Yom Kippur War was also the culmination of Israel's history of large force-on-force wars. From that moment on, the character of the defense of Israel changed from a small David surrounded by Goliaths, to that of fragile stability. The peace talks following the war provided that measure of security, Israel's infant nuclear program provided additional deterrence, and the US involvement added an extra layer of certainty on it. Israel was no longer alone in negotiating and deterring its neighbor-enemies. As a nation, Israel had the breathing room to recover from the losses of the Yom Kippur War and humbly move forward in planning and posturing for its future defense. More importantly, with its immediate borders at less of a risk of a major attack, Israel could shift its focus from its immediate neighborhood to further out into the region to address threats.

---

[60] Rodman, *Sword and Shield of Zion : The Israel Air Force in the Arab-Israeli Conflict, 1948-2012.*

Chapter 4

A New Era in David's Air Force, 1973-1985

The Zionist entity [Israel] understands that one of the most decisive factors in determining the future of the conflict the Arab nation is waging against it is the continued presence of the technical and scientific gap between it and the Arab nation. Therefore, it [Israel] is trying by all means to keep this gap within limits which will not enable the Arab nation to achieve victory over it in the conflict.

- Official statement published by the Iraqi government on June 8, 1981, following the attack on its nuclear reactor complex

Introduction

The political and military actions did not stop with the exact end of the Yom Kippur War. Although the war began with a surprise to Israel that had distressing effects on its forces, the Israel Defense Forces (IDF) were able to regroup and mitigate the territorial and operational losses. After two rounds of ceasefires, negotiations began between the major participants in the war. The Israeli forces had pushed south to within 101 kilometers of Cairo and north to within 45 kilometers of Damascus. In January 1974, Israel and Egypt signed a disengagement agreement, and five months later in May, Syria followed suit regaining a small piece of the Golan Heights.[1] This set the stage for the 1978 Camp David accords eventually return the Sinai to Egypt and facilitate an Israeli peace with Egypt and eventually Jordan. Although a proper peace with Syria did not come to fruition, the Syrian military was sufficiently weakened to no longer pose as severe a threat to Israel as it once had.

The end of the Yom Kippur War marked a new era for the state of Israel. It would be the last in its history of large force-on-force wars and would represent the dawn of the era of Israeli counterterrorism and asymmetric operations. No longer would Israel's immediate neighbors represent an ongoing existential threat, but rather, with the relative stability that sprouted from the Yom Kippur War ceasefire and negotiations, that threat was now elsewhere. The threats to the Jewish state came in many forms. Anti-Zionist terrorist

---
[1] Ahron Bregman, *Israel's Wars*, 2016, 147.

groups arose out of popular anger from the Arab détente with Israel, with many in the Arab world perceiving it as another humiliating failure.

Additionally, other Arab and Muslim states throughout the Middle East and Northern Africa, having not faced Israel in direct combat, maintained destructive and aggressive rhetoric against it. Actions deliberately crafted to undermine the fragile stability in the area accompanied these official threats and words of hatred. For example, some governments sponsored terrorist groups, or sought to strike fear in the hearts of the Jewish state's citizens, or pursued nuclear weapons to finally rid the Middle East of this "problem."

The distancing of the sources of danger from the Israeli borders outwards allowed Israeli leaders to raise their eyes to the horizon and consider how to approach those problems from afar. The Israeli state's goals had not changed despite over thirty years of fighting; it simply wanted to survive, but preferably live in relative peace and security. The threat of terrorist action at home and abroad against Israeli citizens and assets grew, and those who would do harm to Israel continued pursuing capabilities that could destroy the young nation. Thus, the Israeli leaders charged the IDF to posture and position themselves to secure Israeli interests and persons, beyond mere national survival, at any cost at home and abroad. This charge is evident when examining several Israeli Air Force (IAF) actions in the next decade as the IAF executed operations in Uganda, Lebanon, Iraq, and Tunisia. More importantly, during this time, the IAF would become a strategic tool of national power in the face of varying threats to Israeli national security.

An Air Force in Transition

The Yom Kippur War represented a turning point in the IDF and IAF's history. The lessons derived from the War of Attrition leading into the Yom Kippur War would propel them both on a different trajectory. The IDF writ large was well versed in the tactical debrief to learn all lessons from a given encounter. The Yom Kippur War was also evaluated in this line of thought, except with extra emphasis added upon it by the IAF. The IAF conducted numerous investigations and evaluations to identify the flaws and gaps of its performance in that disastrous war. All inquiries resulted in two major findings: the IAF had failed at its two core areas due both political and military reasons. It had not acted as a preemptive and preventative force prior to the war, and it had not won the air war. These reflections accompanied a returned feeling of vulnerability and ill-preparedness. The IAF's Commander, Major General Benny Peled, launched a service-wide reorganization.[2]

One lesson was that the IAF could not create plans that relied solely on a preemptive attack. Although this still represented an ideal scenario, the more realistic course of action was to plan for a variety of different scenarios and be ready for any combat event. A second was that unless the whole IAF were fully mobilized and on alert, it would be unrealistic to expect an instantaneous and full IAF response to support requests from the IDF staff. Additionally, pilots learned to swallow their pride as traditional fighter pilots and learn to rely on electronic warfare and munitions that expanded the scope of the fight outside the limits of human sight. The stigma associated with firing air-to-air missiles had to be discarded at the cost of pilot ego to enable a higher success and survivability rate in these critical aircraft.[3]

In the area of munitions, for example, the Israeli-adapted Shrike missiles also underwent upgrades. Initially functioning much like an American HARM missile, targeting radar emanations, the Yom Kippur War showed gaps in its capabilities. Research went into understanding how to target surface-to-air missile systems when the radars were not emanating, a gap in fighter-bomber tactics and capabilities in the Yom Kippur War. Additionally, time, money, and research were dedicated to bettering tracking and targeting methods for mobile surface-to-air missile systems, electronic warfare, computers for flight control in complex electronic environments, and long-range missiles. The IAF operated within a new paradigm. With available resources, it was critical to select the weapons and aircraft that could deliver the greatest damage with the least amount of dedicated resources;[4] in other words, the proverbial biggest bang for the buck.

The simplest changes came in the form of reorganization. The most obvious change to the IAF commander was the need for unique intelligence support to the IAF. It could no longer rely on the intelligence support that it had received from the ground-focused IDF Intelligence Branch. The IAF operated at a different speed, and with different needs. It needed specialized intelligence to support air operations, thus establishing an autonomous

---

[2] His full given name was Benyamin Weidenfeld.
[3] Eliezer Cohen, *Israel's Best Defense* (New York: Orion Books, 1993), 398.
[4] Cohen, 399.

IAF branch supporting air intelligence requirements.[5] Beginning with a leadership change in the intelligence branch, these actions and process changes also tightened the loop for information and intelligence processing, enabling IAF intelligence analysts to examine the aerial reconnaissance and photography that its pilots collected before dissemination to the rest of the IDF.

Additionally, the anti-aircraft artillery units were removed from the ground forces and subordinated to the IAF. This also meant they now came under the efficiency and quality demands that formed Tolkosvki's legacy, in that they would have to train and respond to a higher standard. Additionally, with this all under the umbrella of the IAF, they were better able to ascertain the gaps in capabilities and coverage and attain the best systems to mitigate those risks revealed during combat in 1973.[6]

Also, the use of unmanned aerial vehicles (UAV) proved their worth through the War of Attrition and into the Yom Kippur War. Although initially used as decoys to confuse enemy defenses, it was quickly understood that they also were better used as intelligence, surveillance, and reconnaissance platforms. For similar quality photography and data, they could be employed for a fraction of the cost, both financial and human, with minimum risk to the aircrew.[7]

The IAF took to conducting joint training with the IDF ground forces in an effort to increase interoperability and joint efficacy. It even took to sending air liaison officers to ground units to enhance communications. From these efforts, forward control centers were established to help guide air support operations, and IAF leadership challenged the prioritization and value of the concept of close air support. Although the IDF ground forces were accustomed to calling in fires when they had troops in contact, IAF commander Peled pushed battlefield interdiction and ground attack before the troops came into contact, limiting the risk of fratricide and decreasing limitations on pilots conducting those strikes.

The final series of changes that were born of the Yom Kippur War was in the command and control of air operations. After the disorganization and confusion of the Yom Kippur War, IAF leaders realized that something needed to be done to streamline command

---

[5] Cohen, 400.
[6] Cohen, 430.
[7] Cohen, 429.

and control of air operations. They learned that they needed a clear picture of both air and ground operations to guide their relatively few assets for more effective use. The change to command and control of air assets would be reliant on intelligence, surveillance, and reconnaissance assets that could provide an up-to-date operating picture for the commander of the air war. Second, there had to be a sufficient communications infrastructure that could support the data and visualization requirements of these commanders. This way leaders could more easily keep a finger on the pulse of the air battle as well as direct the air scheme of maneuver.

The IAF placed additional emphasis in its training for strike missions. As has been explained, the IAF had long been subordinated to the immediate needs of the IDF ground forces and was not provided many opportunities to strike targets deep into enemy territory. This was rectified following the Yom Kippur War. The IAF was soon training, and placing a high priority on attack missions and long-range strike missions.[8] These were further enabled by the expansion of the airborne command and control of air operations with purchase and integration of the Hawkeye E-2C aircraft, an airborne command, control, and coordination platform that could centrally monitor, deconflict, and direct aircrew and missions from within or near the area of operations. Thus, technology acquisition and development were driven by, and an influencing factor for, the evolution of IAF doctrine and its updated, prioritized mission sets of deep strike, interdiction, and CAS.

In addition to breathing room to refine tactical and operational aspects of the force, doctrine, and personnel, the ceasefire and peace agreements that culminated the Yom Kippur War had even broader implications. They placed Israel in a heretofore unfamiliar situation. For the first time since its establishment, Israel was not under immediate threat from a neighboring nation-state. Instead, it could lift its eyes to the horizon and past its neighbors to possible threats from further abroad. Unfortunately, Israel still did not have far to look, for the very agreements that guaranteed security from neighbors sparked life in terrorist groups that took up the charge that their countries abandoned. This opened an era of terrorist attacks, actions, and threats that would color Israel's history until the present day.

---

[8] Uri Bar-Joseph, Amos Perlmutter, and Michael I. Handel, *Two Minutes Over Baghdad*, Second (New York: Routledge Taylor & Francis Group, 2003), 97.

A Story of Mobility: Operation Thunderbolt[9]

Although terrorism is a common occurrence today, such acts were novel and unexpected in the 1970s. The Israeli people became the target of attacks, kidnapping, and angry rhetoric. In 1972, the Palestinian Black September Organization hijacked a passenger airliner traveling from Brussels to Israel via Vienna, Sabena Airline's Flight 571. The pro-Palestinian hijackers instructed the pilots to land the plane at Lod airport near Tel Aviv (later to be renamed to Ben Gurion Airport) so that they could make their demands directly to the Israeli government. In exchange for the lives of the passengers, they demanded the release of several hundred Palestinians incarcerated in Israeli jails. Israel responded swiftly with a successfully executed rescue operation utilizing the *Sayeret Matkal,* a special forces entity known as "The Unit." The terrorist groups observed this response to the operation in particular and updated their plans and tactics for future operations.[10]

Four years later, pro-Palestinian terrorists executed what they viewed as a foolproof plan. Two Popular Front for the Liberation of Palestine (PFLP) members and two Revolutionary Cell members hijacked an Air France flight to Paris from Israel via Athens on June 27, 1976. Midflight, the hijackers took control of the plane via physical threat and ordered the pilots to change course. Rather than fly northwest towards Paris, they turned south back over the Mediterranean. The Israeli authorities hoped to lure the hijackers back to Israel where they had more options to defuse the situation. Instead, the hijackers ordered a landing in Benghazi, Libya, for refueling, during which time the passengers were kept on the plane.[11]

At this point, the Israeli government was well aware of the situation. The Prime Minister called for emergency cabinet meetings to understand what was happening and begin the brainstorming for solutions. Benghazi was only three hours' flight time from Lod airport, and there was still a hope of bringing the plane back to Israeli soil. All the members of the Cabinet who remembered how the Sabena situation had culminated years earlier were hopeful for a similar resolution. Thus, they ordered "The Unit" to begin preparations

---

[9] This operation is identified by its official operational code name: Operation Thunderbolt, but is often is referred to as Operation Jonathan after the loss of "The Unit's" commander in execution of the assault, or as Operation Entebbe for the location of the operation.
[10] Saul David, *Operation Thunderbolt: Flight 139 and the Raid on Entebbe Airport, the Most Audacious Hostage Rescue Mission in History* (New York: Little, Brown, 2015), 18.
[11] David, 42.

for a successful repeat of the earlier operation. The deputy commander of "The Unit," Muki Betser, in the absence of the commander, drew up plans and began preparations.[12] However, he knew better than to believe that the same tactics would be successful twice. In his mind, the terrorists would know better than to put themselves in the same situation. Moreover, though he made his opinion known on this topic, he continued to prepare his men for the possibility of a repeat of the Sabena operation;[13] storming the aircraft locally should the plane land on Israeli soil.

Despite their hopes, there would be no repeat of 1972. By Monday, June 28, 1976, the Air France flight had taken off and landed once more, this time in Entebbe, Uganda, southwest of its capital Kampala. From the passengers' accounts, it appeared that the hijackers and the Ugandan soldiers that greeted the aircraft with guns in hand were cooperating. The passengers were moved from the aircraft to the old terminal building on Entebbe Airport, while the Air France jet was moved a "safe" distance away. They would see additional PFLP members join the original hijacking crew in maintaining control over the passengers. Within days, the passengers would be divided into groups. Those with Israeli or apparent Jewish ties were isolated further into the terminal, in even less acceptable conditions. The anticipation of the outcome of this terrorist action was difficult for the hostages and planners alike.

Within the Israeli parliament, the uncertainty of the situation due to numerous variables and lack of information was causing friction among the members and supporting IDF branches. Often based on personal experience, all members of the Israeli authorities had an opinion on terrorism, hijacking, and what the risks were worth. Thus, the debates were colored by personal bias, morality, and politics in addition to searching for an acceptable and reliable resolution. The debates grew hottest between the Prime Minister and the Defense Minister. Prime Minister Yitzhak Rabin, as the head of the Israeli government, baselined expectations for governmental action and approval when he stated his stance on the topic:

---

[12] At this time, Lt Col Yoni Netanyahu, the commander of "The Unit" was conducting training with the unit in the field.
[13] David, *Operation Thunderbolt: Flight 139 and the Raid on Entebbe Airport, the Most Audacious Hostage Rescue Mission in History*, 45.

> When it comes to negotiating with terrorists...I long ago made a decision of principle, well before I became prime minister, that if a situation were ever to arise when terrorists would be holding our people hostage on foreign soil and we were faced with an ultimatum either to free killers in our custody or let our own people be killed, I would, in the absence of a military option, give in to the terrorists. I would free killers to save our people. So I say now, if the defense minister and the chief of staff cannot come up with a credible military plan, I intend to negotiate with the terrorists. I would never be able to look a mother in the eye if her hostage soldier or child, or whoever it was, was murdered because of a refusal to negotiate, or because of a botched operation.[14]

Defense Minister Shimon Peres, on the other hand, commented in retrospect that the question was less in the cost of Israeli lives over terrorist lives, and more so the principle and historical precedent with which the Israeli government and world would then have to endure should they negotiate with the terrorists. He stated, "it became clear to me that we faced, fundamentally, a question of principle. If we were unable to rescue the hostages, our only alternative was to negotiate their release, ultimately giving in to the demands of terrorists. This, I feared, would create a terrible precedent with unknown consequences."[15]

Without a solid plan, the concessions to the terrorists would have rippling effects globally. In his analysis of the Israeli government's predicament, Peres wrote in his biography "If we give in to the hijackers' demands and release terrorists, everyone will understand us, but no one will respect us… If, on the other hand, we conduct a military operation to free hostages, it is possible that no one will understand us-but everyone will respect us."[16] Peres was looking to a future in which terrorists could look back on the Air France hijacking with pride and hope for subsequent success. His goal was to communicate the message to the world that Israel would never allow terrorists (and hijackers) to succeed and survive. Instead, he aimed to turn Entebbe into another deterrent for future action against the Jewish state. This would also double as the torch by which other nations could light the way for future dealings with terrorism.[17]

---

[14] David, 110.
[15] Shimon Peres, *No Room for Small Dreams: Courage, Imagination and the Making of Modern Israel* (UK: Hachette, 2017), 111.
[16] Peres, 111.
[17] Peres, 111.

At nine in the evening on June 29th, Peres called a meeting of his service chiefs looking for options to fix this situation. Although this was the first official meeting on the topic, the IAF Chief, Major General Peled, had already ordered his planners to start their work. As a testament to the training and forward-leaning attitude of the IAF, its planners had unofficially been examining the situation for over a day when that call came in. Thus, their chief was armed for the first meeting.

The planners of all the services were given the objective of "rescue the hostages and exterminate the terrorists and anyone who disrupts the execution of the operation."[18] Going first and representing the IAF's plans, Peled recommended flying to Entebbe and dropping hundreds, if not a thousand, paratroopers in order to secure the airport and surrounding neighborhood. Should they want to control all of Uganda, Peled asserted they would need another thousand soldiers. Initially, these plans were viewed as "fantastic" and dismissed for more practical and credible Israeli Naval Forces (INF) plans. The INF plans contained options for a seaborne attack on Entebbe, delivery of commandos to the airport by airdropped Zodiac, or by troops crossing from Kenya via the water of Lake Victoria.[19] Further discussions on the topic were fraught with doubt and variables that could lead to utter failure. Without a cohesive idea or solution to unify the Israeli government and IDF in its operational planning, the hijackers had succeeded in not only dividing the hostages in the terminal, but the Israeli government as well.

The hijackers' demands, as transmitted on July 1st, complicated the possibility of negotiation and fulfillment by Israel. On that day, the hijackers officially broadcast their demands over the Ugandan radio. They demanded that "freedom fighters" (from varied groups) imprisoned in West Germany, Kenya, Switzerland, France, and Israel be released within 48 hours and flown via Air France to Entebbe.[20] This was in addition to monetary demands. The ability to successfully satisfy these demands was complicated by the transnational and trans-organizational nature of the request. It was a set-up for failure.

On June 30th, the IDF planners met with Major General Peled to review additional options. In 24 hours, the joint planning working group had identified gaps in their

---

[18] David, *Operation Thunderbolt: Flight 139 and the Raid on Entebbe Airport, the Most Audacious Hostage Rescue Mission in History*, 140.
[19] David, 114.
[20] David, 96.

intelligence but still were able to create four distinct options for the general. The intelligence gap whose answer could propel or disassemble the planning options was: *What was Idi Amin's role in all this?* An understanding of the Ugandan stance on the hijacking could mean the difference between a combined Israeli-Ugandan operation (best-case), a Ugandan supported operation (most realistic case), a Ugandan ignored operation, or a Ugandan contested operation (worst case).[21] To their credit, in the absence of this bit of intelligence, the planners were still able to create a range of options.

One option was a joint operation between the IAF's mobility fleet, the IDF ground force's "The Unit", and the INF's naval equivalent, *Shayetet* 13. The second option proposed bringing a joint assault force to Kenya and launching an operation from there. The third option included sending a force to Entebbe in disguise, and launching a surprise attack from within the airport.[22] The last option called for C-130 Hercules cargo planes transporting an assault force to Entebbe and landing there. In that way, the rescued hostages could then fly away to safety on the very same airplanes that brought the assault force there.[23]

The situation changed only marginally over the next few days. Through purported negotiations with the PFLP by Idi Amin on behalf of foreign governments, some hostages were released and others' living conditions were improved. At the same time, the IDF planners continued leveraging the span of IDF assets and capabilities to fill in gaps in their information and plans. Still, the debate raged on internally within parliament. The government had not found an acceptable resolution despite modernizing, improving, and refocusing the IDF to new levels and capabilities. As Peres once wrote:

> The challenges this [situation] presented were enormous. In the aftermath of the 1973 war, Rabin and I had worked to modernize and replenish our military, and to prepare it for the "long arm" option-an ability to strike targets far beyond our immediate horizon. However, no country or army had ever contemplated a challenge of this dimension. It was going to require a military operation to take place thousands of miles away, against armed terrorists and, perhaps, the Ugandan army-all carried out with suboptimal

---

[21] David, 122.
[22] Even the aircraft carrying the military members were to be disguised as a commercial airliner.
[23] David, *Operation Thunderbolt: Flight 139 and the Raid on Entebbe Airport, the Most Audacious Hostage Rescue Mission in History*, 118.

intelligence, against a ticking clock. Most of our senior military leadership seemed to feel that a military rescue operation was simply impossible.[24]

For once, the IAF was not the reverse salient factor in the operational planning. The trust in the capabilities of the IAF was not in question for the "long arm" option ability; rather it was the assault forces' ability to execute the mission within the established accepted risk parameters.

The ticking clock was the worst aspect of the situation. If a solution were possible, most on the planning teams felt that they could find it. However, operational time constraints changed the landscape of the possible. After several meetings that day on June 30, 1976, a trio of officers conceptualized yet another plan to rescue the hostages.[25] They adapted a previous plan, envisioning two refueling C-130 airplanes with the range to fly to Uganda, landing on the new runway at Entebbe in the cover of darkness. From the bellies of the C-130s would emerge a smaller assault force in "innocent-looking vehicles" to surprise the terrorists in the Old Terminal, successfully extinguishing the threat and rescuing the hostages. Then they would all return via the C-130s in which they arrived.[26] When pitched to Colonel Shai Tamari, the deputy chief of the Special Operations Division, the impression was that the plan was vague but held promise, and they were directed to explore this option further.

Nevertheless, exploring options, deciding on operations, posturing assets, and executing an operation takes time. Time was not on their side. These discussions were taking place within hours of the ultimatum deadline. So it was that Prime Minister Rabin held his own meeting, and garnered a consensus to push forward with negotiating with the hijackers through France. Shortly afterward, it was broadcasted by the PFLP that they shifted the deadline to Sunday, July 4, 1976. Israel now had the time to rescue its people and neutralize this threat, although many of its civilian leaders were still skeptical of the plan coming together.

By mid-afternoon on July 1, the planners were narrowing down the specifics of the operation. While the special forces planners from "The Unit" were figuring out the assault,

---

[24] Peres, *No Room for Small Dreams: Courage, Imagination and the Making of Modern Israel*, 110.
[25] David, *Operation Thunderbolt: Flight 139 and the Raid on Entebbe Airport, the Most Audacious Hostage Rescue Mission in History*, 158.
[26] David, 147.

IAF planners were determining the discrete airlift requirements to enable the entire operation. They arrived at a force of five C-130 cargo planes (with one as a reserve). The initial assault crews would be delivered with the first aircraft. The second plane would contain reinforcements. The third and fourth planes would also contain more equipment and reinforcements, but also a medical crew with a configuration to treat up to seventy-five casualties. The plan called for less than ten minutes of combat, but the fueling limitation of the C-130s on this long haul would require a refueling on the ground in Entebbe, which they planned to do with mobile hand-operated pumps they would bring along.[27]

Much of the popularized story of the Entebbe operation focuses on the bravery, skill, and preparation of the men of "The Unit" as they trained and executed the operation. They earned that fame and awe. However, the men of the IAF that crewed those C-130 airplanes spent equal time training for actions that had never been accomplished before, convincing their leadership that they were up to the task of delivering "The Unit" and returning home with everyone safely.

The pilots had to demonstrate to the Israeli Chief of Staff Motta Gur and IAF Chief Benny Peled that they were able to land their aircraft safely while essentially "blind." One of the deal-breakers on this mission for the decisionmakers was the guarantee that just the landing in Entebbe could be accomplished. There were concerns that the runway lights would be off, and so the pilots would have to rely solely on the radar in the plane, the Adverse Weather Aerial Delivery System, that was designed for blackout landings.[28] After two nerve-wracking but satisfactory demonstrations, they were cleared to fly the mission.

The IAF planners were thorough. Every detail was calculated and accounted for from pounds of fuel, travel time, routes, command and control aircraft, and backup plans to backup plans. They also planned to preposition a full medical outfit and plane in Kenya where the Israeli government had secured a refueling and a stopover point for after the operation. The pilots continued to practice their landings and study the routes. The assault forces ran drills in mock-ups of the terminal building. By the end of July 2, 1976, all that was left to launch the operation was the authority to do so. Rabin was slow to provide his approval, but in a cabinet meeting the morning of Saturday, July 3, 1976, he authorized the

---

[27] David, 192.
[28] David, 245.

assets to be prepositioned at the appropriate starting points of the mission in the Sinai.[29] Later that day, Rabin briefed the entire cabinet to garner a consensus to authorize the full operation.

At 1:55PM on July 3, 1976, the fully laden Hercules airplanes took off from Lod airport. The observant passerby would not know the planes were rendezvousing later, because all the planes took off towards different directions as a distraction and precaution. Shortly before takeoff, Israeli intelligence was able to hand-deliver updated overhead imagery of the Entebbe airport, taken by camera from an IAF light aircraft. The imagery was both timely and useful in filling some of the gaps that had remained in the assault force's plan.[30] The planes continued their flight towards the Sinai at merely a few hundred feet off the ground to evade detection of Jordanian and Soviet radar.[31]

Once the planes and crews had refueled and rested at Ofira air base in the Sinai, they were quickly loaded up again. They had received the authorization to conduct the operation and were quick not to lose any more time. Fully laden, the cargo planes strained to take flight, and by 7:55 pm Israeli-time soon carrying the long-arm of Israeli justice to Entebbe.

As the first C-130 airplane approached the Entebbe airport, the crew lowered its rear ramp a little to save time on the ground launching the assault force. The pilot was relieved to see the runway lights still on and executed a flawless landing. Seconds later, the assault forces drove towards the terminal and the rescue. Next, as the plane slowed down, other soldiers aboard jumped out to emplace battery-operated lanterns on either side of the runway. This would act as emergency landing lights if the Ugandan control tower team turned off the runway lights. This precaution would prove unnecessary as the C-130s would catch the Ugandans entirely by surprise.

As the operation unfolded on the ground, the aircrew was refueling their planes by hand-operated pumps and preparing for the evacuation. When the teams began to return with the wounded, dead, and ambulatory, medical teams jumped into action. Unfortunately, they were unable to save all who were brought to them. Instead, they loaded up the rescued

---

[29] David, 266.
[30] David, 271.
[31] At the time of the operation, Soviet ships were anchored nearby and able to detect the aircraft should they fly within the line of sight of the radar.

hostages on the planes and readied for takeoff. The hand-operated pumps did not work as well as they had needed, so the crew took off towards Kenya to use El-Al Airline resources there, and bring the wounded to the medical team awaiting them.[32]

It was now around lunchtime on July 4, 1976, and the Israeli government, family, and friends greeted their rescued citizens as they landed in Lod Airport. At approximately 5:45PM of the same day, the Prime Minister had announced the rescue in a special gathering of the Israeli Knesset. The operation and homecoming were celebrated throughout the country and much of the free world. Through the use of air mobility as a strategic enabler, the Israelis were able to defend their interests and security practically a world away. What is more, the quality of the aircrews in maintaining and flying the planes was critical to the success of the operation.

Overall, Operation Thunderbolt's success set the precedent that Shimon Peres envisioned. It was the role model action for most Western governments in response to a hostage-taking situation. In doing so, it realigned governmental preferences from negotiation to military counter-strike capabilities, even prompting the establishment of special Israeli counter-terrorist units in various countries. Israel had shown that there was no profit in hijacking and hostage-taking. Later, Germany would follow in their footsteps, ordering its GSG-9 commandos to assault a plane which had been hijacked in Mogadishu. The GSG-9 are the German Federal Police special commando unit tasked with counterterrorism and other specialized missions.[33] Also, the US would look to Operation Thunderbolt when faced with a hostage situation at the American Embassy in Tehran, Iran, going so far as to call Israeli parliament members for advice. Unfortunately, the US Operation Eagle Claw did not have as successful ending as the Israeli operation. Regardless, in one operation, the Israelis were able to change the counterterrorism fight and the West's paradigm of dealing with violent, non-state groups.

This precedent-setting operation would not have been possible had it not been for visionary leadership affecting change within the Israeli government and IDF. When

---

[32] David, *Operation Thunderbolt: Flight 139 and the Raid on Entebbe Airport, the Most Audacious Hostage Rescue Mission in History*, 313.
[33] "Federal Police - GSG 9 Der Bundespolizei," accessed April 25, 2019, https://web.archive.org/web/20160522195149/http://www.bundespolizei.de/Web/DE/05Die-Bundespolizei/04Einsatzkraefte/03GSG9/GSG9_node.html.

Yitzhak Rabin and Shimon Peres were staff members in the Israeli government pursuing the modernization of the IAF, they did not know explicitly what the future IAF would have to accomplish. Instead, they had a vision of an air force able to extend its support and effect from the traditional tactical to a more strategic and long-reaching capability. It was their nascent air-mindedness or belief in airpower that enabled Operation Thunderbolt and subsequent operations. The Lebanon War was a convergence of state and non-state actors threatening Israel, and another opportunity for the IAF to demonstrate its utility in a new and strategic context.

The First Lebanon War

When Israel invaded Lebanon in the early 1980s, it was with the intent to destroy the terrorist organizations that were taking sanctuary in the country and conducting attacks against IDF soldiers on and around the border. The goal was to deny the terrorists' ability to rebuild and regroup. In this way, the operations in Lebanon were described by Ariel Sharon as a method by which to establish a new political order in Lebanon, primarily by destroying the terrorist organizations present.[34] The Israeli leadership elected to counter the terrorist attacks with an air-centric coercive strategy of both retaliatory and preemptive strikes.[35]

The IAF was already familiar with the situation on the ground and in the air surrounding Lebanon. As Lebanon became an arena for groups and states seeking to gain influence over the area, Israel soon stepped in. More than unwanted instability on its northern border, Israeli officials identified anti-Zionist and anti-Israeli groups that were establishing their own sanctuaries from which to attack Israel.[36] Additionally, circumstances were such that Syria became involved in Lebanon, leading the IAF and Syrian Air Forces to clash sporadically in air-to-air combat. However, the IAF's newer, stronger, faster, and better-trained force was able to meet the IDF's needs.

When the cost of Israeli blood became too high, and a myriad of anti-war protests began to plague the nation, the Israeli leadership ordered a redeployment of troops to the so-called Awali Line of outposts and fortifications. This redeployment was intended to

---

[34] Zeev Schif and Ehud Ya'ari, "Israel's Lebanon War", p.42-43.
[35] Kenneth C. Show Jr, "Falcons Against Jihad" (Air University, 1995), 4.
[36] Anti-Zionism refers to a sentiment against the Jewish movement for self-determination and the establishment of a Jewish state. Anti-Israeli refers to a deep criticism of the state of Israel and its policies.

open up the door for negotiations and reduce future attacks; it did not work. Instead, the IAF was selected to take up the strike role in dealings with the terrorist organizations in Lebanon. To do this properly, it would need to leverage all available capabilities its inventory held (see Table 6.)

On 3 November 1983, the IAF struck its first terrorist targets in Alley, Bhamdoun, and Sofar. "This raid would mark the beginning of Israel's use of air power to support their efforts to control the behavior of the Palestinian and Lebanese organizations during this period."[37] Israel had applied the same logic and mindset for utilization of airpower against terrorist threats in this scenario as it had when it developed the strategy initially in 1966, and as such an IAF retaliatory air raid was not an uncommon occurrence. The increasing commonality of these strikes had a lesser psychological effect on the Palestinian and Lebanese terrorist groups than the Israeli leaders had hoped.

The IAF employed its most modern aircraft in its efforts against the terrorist groups: A-4, F-4E, F-15, F-16, and Kfir aircraft. These aircraft and the IAF system supporting the surgical strikes operated beautifully; executing operations that successfully destroyed targets while limiting civilian casualties. An interesting aspect of these air raids was that the formulation of strategy and target selection was kept in the hands of the Israeli Prime Minister and his cabinet.[38] Despite the handpicked targets, the strikes were not achieving the desired effects. The IAF turned to more night sorties in hopes of gaining the element of surprise, but still, the successfully executed operations were not culminating in the coercive effects that were conceived by the Israeli leadership. In further attempts to gain the element of surprise, the IAF selected the AH-1S Cobra and Hughes 500 MD Defender helicopters for night time raids. In addition to executing the targeting operations themselves, the helicopters were used to deliver specially trained platoons of paratroopers to execute ground raids as well.[39]

---

[37] Show Jr, "Falcons Against Jihad.", 5.
[38] Show Jr., 6.
[39] Show Jr., 7.

Table 6. IAF starting inventory in 1978.

Aircraft	Aircraft Type	Number of Aircraft
F-15E Eagles	Multirole	25
F-4E Phantom II	Fighter-bombers	204
RF-4E	Reconnaissance fighters	12
Dassault Mirage II CJ	Interceptors	50
Neshers (Israeli built Mirages with Atar engine)	Fighter-bombers	50
IAI Kfirs	Fighter-bombers	50
Dassault Mystere IV	Fighter-bombers	25
Dassault Ouragons	Fighter-bombers	25
A-4E/H/M/N Skyhawks	Attack aircraft	250+ (and 24 trainers)
Vautours	Attack aircraft	10
Fouga Magister	Trainer	80
Lockheed C-130E	Transport aircraft	12
Lockheed C-130H	Transport aircraft	12
Lockheed KC-130H	Aerial Tankers	2
Boeing 707-320	Transport aircraft	5
Boeing C-97	Transport aircraft	12
Nord Noratlas	Transport aircraft	20
Douglas C-47 Dakotas	Transport aircraft	10
Sud Super Frelons	Rotary wing	12
Sikorsky S-65 C-3 and CH-53G	Rotary wing	15
Bell 205	Rotary wing	23
Bell UH-1D	Rotary wing	20+
Alouette II and III	Rotary wing	12
Sikorsky S-61R	Rotary wing	12
Boeing Vertol CH-47C	Rotary wing	12
Beech Modele 80 Queen Air	Light Aircraft	20
Britten-Norman Islanders	Light Aircraft	12
Dornier Do 27	Light Aircraft	10
Dornier Do 28	Light Aircraft	10
IAI Arava 201	Light Aircraft	14
Cessna 206C Super Skywagon	Light Aircraft	5
IAI Westwing	Light Aircraft	3
Piper Super Cubs	Light Aircraft	20
Grumman E-2C Hawkeyes	Early Warning Aircraft	4

Source: Adapted from Rubenstein's Shield of David.

Overall, the efforts of the IAF during this operation were not nearly as impressive as in previous wars. During this time, the IAF would fly less than ten missions per month, allowing of the coercive diplomacy strategy to work. As a point of comparison, the total number of missions flown between January 1983 and June 1985 in Lebanon was less than that of the first day of the 1967 war.[40]

A point of contention in history is whether the air strikes against Lebanon were effective. Ultimately, it is a matter of examining it at different levels of war. Tactically, the Israeli government's public affairs department termed the raids a success, citing successful sorties and targets destroyed. However, strategically, the strikes were ineffective. They did not stop the terrorist violence against IDF troops in that region.[41] The IAF was not at fault for this failure, but rather the civilian leaders misunderstood the nature of the conflict and how the application of airpower would affect the desired outcome. This was difficult for leaders to learn and understand. In their minds, they had the most capable and technologically advanced air force in the region. Additionally, they were fighting against guerrilla forces with little resources on their side. This time, Israel was the Goliath to the terrorist David, and yet, they were not able to win. The Israeli leaders learned an important lesson that had been forgotten by the corporate government, that "technology and size does not guarantee "coercive" victories."[42]

Beyond the persistent threat of terrorism to the Israeli government and people, the Israeli leaders were still leery of the fragile peace in the region. The Israeli intelligence apparatus worked hard to identify potential threats in its immediate vicinity and abroad. The modernization of weaponry and proliferation of weapons of mass destruction became a topic of interest because of the asymmetric force qualities and potential for unbalancing the military balance of power in the region.

Operation Babylon: The Attack on Osirak, the Iraqi Nuclear Reactor

The Israelis first discovered Iraqi nuclear development operations in 1978 when Iranian sources loyal to the Shah provided intelligence to the US and Israeli governments. However, the threat did not reach such a level that the Israelis were moved to military

---

[40] Show Jr, 21.
[41] Show Jr, "Falcons Against Jihad." 18.
[42] Show Jr. 28.

action, yet. Instead, Israeli leaders elected to observe from a healthy distance, waiting for indications that a comprehensive military action was warranted. Shortly afterward, in 1979, the Iranian White Revolution occurred, and an extremely religious Islamic government under the Ayatollah Khomeini ousted the Shah. Iran and Iraq were soon at war, and the Iranian Air Force attempted a strike at the Iraqi reactor complex. Israeli intelligence discovered improvements to the reactors defensive measures, including being "surrounded by batteries of dirt and by an enormous protective wall, thirty meters high."[43] Additionally, by the end of 1979, SA-6 surface-to-air missile systems and man-portable air defense systems (MANPADS) were positioned around the complex. Helium balloons attached to steel cables floated mercilessly above the reactor, creating obstacles and barriers to low-flying missiles and aircraft.

As time progressed and the Iraqi nuclear program developed further, the Israelis believed that Iraqi leader Saddam Hussein's aggressive rhetoric against them was buoyed by the potential enabler of a nuclear weapon. It was clear that he desired the opportunity and capability to rid the world of the Jewish state, and in Israeli minds the possibility of a nuclear weapon elevated this to a credible existential threat. The flight time from Iraq to Israel would not be long for a fighter plane or bomber. However, that timeline would be even shorter if a weapon was delivered by the SS-21 surface-to-surface missiles that Iraq had purchased from the Soviet Union. Additionally, these missiles had the potential for nuclear configuration. This combination of intent, means, and even a possible timeline was sufficient to send the IDF in November 1979 into planning for a way to mitigate the perceived soon-to-be-realized existential threat. Additionally, there was a concern that Iraq would not only use the weapon themselves but also that they might sponsor a terrorist group with this capability, adding layers of risk and danger.[44]

Hussein had two long-term goals for the Gulf region. The first was for Iraq to replace Iran as the dominant Muslim power in the Persian Gulf. The second goal was the destruction of Israel. In a Baghdad radio speech, Hussein declared "the essence of the Iraqi regime's stand on a total rejection of any political solution. Settlement lies in an all-out

---

[43] Cohen, *Israel's Best Defense*, 447.
[44] Bar-Joseph, Perlmutter, and Handel, *Two Minutes Over Baghdad*, xix.

military struggle, aimed at uprooting Zionism from the area."[45] Hussein saw a nuclear weapon as an enabler to these goals.

Iraq's nuclear project began as a cooperative effort with the USSR to build a small reactor in Al Tawita, twenty kilometers southeast of Baghdad, and was augmented by subsequent agreements with other nations, growing to a dangerous level capable of producing weapons-grade plutonium.[46] By the end of 1976, the Iraqi-French project to build a French-designed reactor in Al Tawita was underway. The Osirak project, as it was named, consisted of two reactors: a seventy-megawatt reactor named Osiris and a smaller research nuclear reactor named Isis. The Iraqis named the entire project *17 Tammuz*, for the 17th day of the month of Tammuz in their calendar. As such, the Osiris reactor was renamed Tammuz 1, and the second was named Tammuz 2. As time progressed, Iraq was able to add Italian contractor scientists to the project crew, further advancing the state's nuclear ambitions and timeline.[47] Israeli intelligence learned from sources that during the summer of 1980, Iraqi scientists projected completion for Project 17 Tammuz within the next year.[48]

In August 1980, the Israeli Cabinet could not reach an agreement on what to do regarding the reactor. Some desired the full use of the military against the target, whereas others did not perceive an urgency based on the latest intelligence reports they received. Thus, the potential cost of such a military operation could far outweigh the potential benefits at that point in time. It was better to plan for delaying the Iraqi program via other means.[49]

The Iranians set a precedent for a preemptive attack against the nuclear reactor, and this emboldened the Israelis. The Iranian strike resulted in minimal damage, setting the program back several months.[50] The strike also boosted Iraqi confidence that their precautions for securing the reactor were sufficient. Fortunately for the Israeli intelligence analysts, the increased protective measures surrounding the reactor building had a

---

[45] Bar-Joseph, Perlmutter, and Handel, 39.
[46] Bar-Joseph, Perlmutter, and Handel, 40–41.
[47] Bar-Joseph, Perlmutter, and Handel, 43.
[48] Bar-Joseph, Perlmutter, and Handel, 48; Malfrid Braut-Hegghammer, *Unclear Physics; Why Iraq and Libya Failed to Build Nuclear Weapons* (Ithaca, NY: Cornell University Press, 2016), 56.
[49] Bar-Joseph, Perlmutter, and Handel, *Two Minutes Over Baghdad*, xxviii.
[50] Braut-Hegghammer, *Unclear Physics; Why Iraq and Libya Failed to Build Nuclear Weapons*, 68.

paradoxical effect. Although physically providing layers of protection, it also provided intelligence analysts with sufficient indicators as to the positioning and importance of the building itself.[51] The Iranian attack of September 30, 1980, did not draw so much international attention that it would deter the Israeli attack from occurring later on. The Iranians were not reprimanded by the international community due to the perception of jus in bello derived from the right to self-defense as victims of unprovoked Iraqi aggression. In Israel's mind, this was a similar situation as to that in which they found themselves. Iraq had supported several wars against Israel with troops and supplies, and it was the sole country to reject the 1973 cease-fire outright. If Iraq was still "at war" with Israel, then this continuation justified the targeting of the reactor as an act of self-defense.[52]

As soon as the Israeli government selected the surgical air strike option over the others that were available at the time (clandestine operation, full-force ground attack, elite team ground assault, etc.) the IAF's planning team went to work. Their intelligence needs had to be met to satisfy planning requirements. The Israeli intelligence community started the dossier on the nuclear plant in 1975 and had kept it updated ever since. Additionally, military intelligence and the Mossad, Israel's intelligence service, worked to close intelligence gaps, specifically targeting human sources that worked in and around the reactor. This effort was rewarded by the French and Italian scientists who provided information shortly after leaving the reactor complex following the Iranian attack in 1980.[53]

After attempting to keep the nuclear threat to Israel out of the national media, the Israeli government eventually allowed the media to take up the issue with full power. The outrage and debate sparked in the press during the summer of 1980 were also picked up by the foreign press as the newest hot topic in the volatile Middle East. This helped to promote the threat of the Iraqi nuclear program internationally and begin to normalize the idea that this would be sufficient casus belli for Israel to strike the reactor, much as the Iranians had just attempted.[54]

Initial planning for the Osiris strike involved a large force of Phantom and Skyhawk aircraft. Additionally, planning was complicated by the need to refuel the aircraft.

---

[51] Cohen, *Israel's Best Defense*, 447.
[52] Bar-Joseph, Perlmutter, and Handel, *Two Minutes Over Baghdad*, xx.
[53] Bar-Joseph, Perlmutter, and Handel, 89.
[54] Bar-Joseph, Perlmutter, and Handel, 60.

Regardless, the IAF planners were able to devise a workable and good plan, though more complicated than they would have liked. However, before the planning efforts were too far along, IAF leaders were informed of a shipment of F-16 aircraft from the US that would arrive earlier than expected. These newer and more modern aircraft also had a longer range, reducing the need for aerial refueling to conduct the mission.[55] Thus, the planning for the mission centered around two four-ship formations of both F-16 and F-15 aircraft.

The F-16 aircraft were planned to fly the whole mission without refueling, enabled by extra gas from their drop tanks. They would be escorted by F-15 aircraft also configured with drop tanks, to provide air-to-air protection.[56] Amid the planning process, the 1976 US elections inadvertently temporarily threatened to alter the conditions and details of the planned mission. US President Jimmy Carter's election worried the Israelis. They did not know the new president's intentions and were nervous that the remainder of the F-16 aircraft delivery would be changed. This turned out to be an unnecessary planning item - the delivery progressed as planned.[57]

Israeli intelligence analysts assessed that the only real concern would be an immediate reaction from the Iraqi military. Thus, the timing of the event would be crucial to several factors, but the highest amongst those was the potential for collateral damage to the outlying community. The strike had to be planned such that the bombing would occur prior to the reactor going "hot," before the production of enriched uranium. Since there would be more trepidation in attacking a hot reactor, the likelihood that the government would call off the strike would rise, providing Iraq the opportunity to weaponize its uranium. By New Year's Eve, 1981, plutonium production started, indicating the nuclear weapons phase was close to fruition. Additionally, Hussein continued to declare his intention of destroying Israel; there was no doubt in Israeli minds that any Iraqi nuclear weapon was meant for use against the Jewish state.[58]

In addition to information regarding the target itself, the IAF intelligence branch worked diligently for a year, collecting, exploiting, and translating information into

---

[55] Cohen, *Israel's Best Defense*, 448.
[56] Use of the drop tanks while armed were against US recommendations; they worried about the risk of a collision between a drop tank and bomb.
[57] Cohen, *Israel's Best Defense*, 446.
[58] Cohen, 450.

intelligence as they examined threats along the route to ensure the survivability of the aircrew and aircraft destined to deliver the fatal blow to the Tammuz reactors. The distance by air from major Israeli air bases to Baghdad was over 1100 kilometers, meaning that this would be "the longest bombing raid in history."[59] Fortunately, the modern and better navigational systems organic to the F-15 and F-16 aircraft would enable a low approach to the target area while still maintaining a needed level of precision and surprise.[60]

Intelligence analysts had assessed that each F-16 had to be armed with two penetration-capable munitions with fuze delays. The bombs would have to enter the target at a forty-five-degree angle through the concrete dome and into the reactor to ensure the most effective placing of the blast within the fortified structure. Also, the timing of the operation was of the utmost importance, and the planners reduced the windows for the bombing run to narrow slits. Each aircraft would have only thirty seconds for its part in the overall operation, an attack that needed to culminate in less than three minutes. Additionally, the pilots were forbidden from taking a second run at the target should they be off on the first run. Last but not least, they could not engage with the Jordanian air force - even if it meant having to abandon the aircraft.[61]

In the midst of the secretive planning and training for the operation, the overall effort met one more delay. Once Prime Minister Begin set a date of May 10, 1981, for the operation, internal tensions ran higher. There was no way to know if there was an information leak within the network and if the IAF could maintain its necessary level of surprise. However, when the opposition party's leader, Shimon Peres, sent a message to Begin strongly urging him to reconsider any use of the military against the nuclear reactor, Begin feared that a leak had occurred and threatened the strike. The mission was postponed to a later day in which the Israeli leadership could be more secure in achieving surprise over the enemy. Ultimately, Prime Minister Begin and the IDF leaders selected June 7, 1981, as the final strike date.[62]

The sophistication of the planning effort and surgical strike encapsulates all the needed aspects of information, intelligence, training, and capabilities needed to make this

---

[59] Bar-Joseph, Perlmutter, and Handel, *Two Minutes Over Baghdad*, 91.
[60] Bar-Joseph, Perlmutter, and Handel, 98.
[61] Cohen, *Israel's Best Defense*, 452.
[62] Cohen, 451–54.

happen. Authors Perlmutter, Handel, and Bar-Joseph explain that the need for secrecy and surprise in this operation was achieved by five overlapping efforts:

> "The first was to choose a course of flight in between enemy radars so that the aircraft would not be detected; the second was to fly as low as possible, so that even if the aircraft were to fly through an area normally covered by radar they would be *below [sic]* the detecting range and level of the radars; the third was the strict maintenance of radio silence; fourth, the blinding of the enemy's radars or, by what is known as ECM or Electronic Counter Measures…; fifth and finally, if the planes were detected in mid-flight the pilots could still avoid identification by direct deception – by pretending that they were Jordanian or Saudi pilots on a training mission, by using clear identification marks and by the passive means of camouflage."[63]

The planning and execution of this operation was masterful work. Each section of the IDF orchestra brought a specific aspect to the musical piece that would sound the destruction of the Iraqi nuclear reactor. The IAF and Israeli Intelligence gathered the parameters and details of the target. Israeli Engineers broke those down into equations driving operational and tactical selections of weaponry, aircraft, and timing. Ultimately planners brought the whole thing together as the conductors of the event. The F-16 aircraft would launch in two formations, each plane carrying a one-ton bomb under each wing and drop tanks to take on the unprecedented 2,500-kilometer round-trip. Once on station, the first bombs would crack open the reactor building from on high. The following bombing runs would ring out as they destroyed the internal contents of the building, smashing floor by floor until even the basement was in shambles and the roof would collapse.

The formations took off from Etzion Air Base near Eilat in the South of Israel. Rather than taking the shortest, most direct route to Al Tawita, the planners plotted a route around Jordan, through Saudi Arabia, and into Iraq. After take-off, the aircraft had a ninety-minute "commute" to and from the target area.[64] In music and military operations, periods of silence have a point. They punctuate the importance of the moment to a listener as much as the moments filled with notes and percussion. It is during these quiet moments that one can reflect on the sounds that passed and those yet to occur. The electronic countermeasures equipment was likely of Israeli manufacture installed on US-made aircraft.[65] It was not

---

[63] Bar-Joseph, Perlmutter, and Handel, *Two Minutes Over Baghdad*, 104.
[64] Cohen, *Israel's Best Defense*, 455.
[65] Bar-Joseph, Perlmutter, and Handel, *Two Minutes Over Baghdad*, 107.

until they were deep within Iraqi radar detection range that the pilots broke radio silence for safety reasons as they closed in on their target area. On final approach, the crew took the aircraft into a climb to ensure the appropriate dive angle to facilitate the munitions' penetration. The eight aircraft executed their maneuvers in five-second intervals. The second formation and did similarly, dropping their bombs into the smoke like the final notes of an etude.[66] Thus, within minutes, the Iraqi nuclear reactor was functionally killed. The understanding of the extent of the damage to the overall program varies between sources. But, it is clear that in the Israeli mind, the operation had negated an imminent existential threat. More recent analysis shows that the Iraqi nuclear program was not as close to weaponization as the Israeli human intelligence sources had indicated.[67]

This operation represented the first successful preemptive strike against a nuclear installation in history.[68] It raised questions regarding strategic deterrence and what conventional military means could mean in that regard. Additionally, experts now wondered at the capabilities that Israel possessed, and its effects on the balance of power and arms races within the Middle East. Lastly, American experts had difficulty accepting that the F-16 aircraft that they had sold to the Israelis had been used in this raid in ways beyond which it had been designed.[69]

For example, the F-16 aircraft had been outfitted with Mark-84 unguided munitions and not precision-guided munitions (PGM) because Israeli planners could not reconcile the PGM required employment parameters with the mission requirements. Despite the use of "dumb" or unguided munitions on this strike, the precision with which it was executed was remarkable. The accuracy of the whole formation's munitions left most analysts and political leaders believing that the IAF had utilized PGMs. But, this level of precision could be attributed to the strict and rigorous training that the F-16 pilots underwent, coupled with the lower altitude from which they launched the bombs.[70]

The political and international fallout from such a strike was not as severe as Israel had expected. Although encouraged by the overall lack of negative international reaction

---

[66] Cohen, *Israel's Best Defense*, 457.
[67] Braut-Hegghammer, *Unclear Physics; Why Iraq and Libya Failed to Build Nuclear Weapons*, 72.
[68] Bar-Joseph, Perlmutter, and Handel, *Two Minutes Over Baghdad*, xvii.
[69] Cohen, *Israel's Best Defense*, 460.
[70] Bar-Joseph, Perlmutter, and Handel, *Two Minutes Over Baghdad*, 115.

to the Iranian attack a year earlier, the context for the Jewish state striking Iraq, rather than a war internal to the Muslim world, made it more prone to a severe reaction and more backlash. However, as it turned out, the Israeli strike was a boon for the remainder of the Middle East. Many Arab governments – and that of Iran - were equally afraid of the possibility of an Iraqi nuclear state as they were of Israel, and were grateful to see that capability disappear. Thus, this cut some of the animosity among the Arab states toward Israel, limiting the reaction to perceptions of the Israeli government attempting to maintain their technical superiority over the Arab states in the region.[71]

The overall importance of this strike on the nuclear reactor would not be realized until two decades had passed. During the Gulf War in 1991, Iraq launched 39 Scud missiles at Israel (and the Kingdom of Saudi Arabia) as the US and its coalition partners sought to drive Iraqi forces out of Kuwait. Iraq was trying to draw Israel into the fight in order to garner more support in its operations against the US. When the citizens of Israel were huddled in their safe rooms with gas masks on, silent thanks were sent up that they were only facing the possibility of a chemical or biological attack, but not one of a nuclear attack.

Whether SCUD missiles, airplanes, or tanks, these weapons and weapon systems represent merely possibilities of action. It is the intent with which they are used that determines the level of effect they are intended to have. They can all be used to create a tactical effect on the battlespace, an operational effect in a battle, or depending on the mode of use and target, a strategic effect across a series of targets, persons, and instruments of power. The strike on the Osirak reactor represented Israel's use of airpower as an instrument of national power as it maintained Israel's continuing advantage in the military and nuclear fields while communicating to the international community a strategic message: we will do what is needed to ensure state survival. As Prime Minister Begin stated in a press conference two days after the strike, "Israel would not under any circumstances permit its enemies to develop weapons of mass destruction."[72]

The Strike on the PLO HQ in Tunisia

State survival continued to be a bifurcated situation in which Israel maintained on eye on nation-states in the region, and on non-state groups which threatened its people. In

---

[71] Bar-Joseph, Perlmutter, and Handel, 169.
[72] Braut-Hegghammer, *Unclear Physics; Why Iraq and Libya Failed to Build Nuclear Weapons*, 73.

1985, the Israeli government was acclimating to the openly asymmetric fight against terrorist organizations. At that time, one of the primary groups on the Israeli radar was the Palestinian Liberation Organization (PLO). Led by its chairman, Yasser Arafat, the PLO conducted and sponsored attacks against the people and government of Israel. After years of IDF and IAF operations against the PLO in Lebanon, many PLO leaders fled from Beirut and took up sanctuary in Tunisia.

The president of Tunisia, Habib Bourgiba, was the sole Arab leader that offered refuge to the PLO as its leaders and members fled the IDF control in Lebanon. The PLO and Force 17, a specialized unit and the PLO's chief operational force following the Lebanon War, established a base of operations in the northern portion of the country along the seacoast. Although it may have afforded them wonderful views, the Hamas A-Shatt neighborhood, twenty kilometers southeast of Tunis, also limited the response time that they and Tunisia could have should any threat approach them from the Mediterranean.

The summer of 1985 brought an increase in the PLO-sponsored and conducted attacks, such that the Israeli government knew it was time to make a declarative statement on the subject. The latest attack, occurring on Yom Kippur, September 25, 1985, involved the murder of three Israelis in the port of Larnaca, Cyprus, and was the final straw for Israel's leaders. Drawing from the state's history of refusing to concede to, or negotiate with terrorists, the Israeli prime minister immediately ordered planning for retaliation. The attack would send a single message the world, for all terrorists and states sponsoring terrorism, to hear: "The IDF will always find and punish those responsible," as Defense Minister Yitzhak Rabin stated.[73]

Israeli intelligence had attributed the increase in attacks against Israel as motivated or sponsored by the PLO. Analysts assessed the assassination in Larnaca to be conducted by Force 17.[74] Although the PLO did not take any formal credit or responsibility for these attacks, the Israeli government relied on its own intelligence that said otherwise.

In late September 1985, the intelligence branches had identified and recommended a PLO target in Tunis, and the IDF recommended to the Minister of Defense that it be

---

[73] "Operation Wooden Leg," accessed November 4, 2019, https://www.idf.il/en/minisites/wars-and-operations/operation-wooden-leg-1985/.
[74] Cohen, *Israel's Best Defense*, 483.

attacked. Unlike the debates that took place before the execution of Operation Thunderbolt, parliament was more prone to agree to this type of operation. Shimon Peres, the Minister of Defense during the planning and execution of Operation Thunderbolt, was now the Prime Minister of Israel. The success of prior operations further cemented his stance of no safe harbor for or negotiation with terrorists. Thus, he was quicker to provide his consent than the debate he experienced in 1976.

After the initial approval for the operation, the IDF selected the IAF as the strike force. The air strike was assessed to have the highest chance of success while posing the lowest risk to the strike force as they conducted this distant operation. The PLO headquarters in Tunis would be the longest range strike the IAF would conduct to date, at approximately 2,400 kilometers. Although the Operation Thunderbolt flight was over 3,200 kilometers, the aircraft used were transports designed for long-distance hauls, and not fighter aircraft designed otherwise. In the years since the rescue from Entebbe, the IAF inventory had continued its modernization. Not only did it now include the fighter aircraft used in the Osirak raid, but also an air-to-air refueling capability.

The IAF fighter pilots spent the majority of the previous ten years practicing aerial refueling and longer-range strikes. This focused mainly on the older model fighters, Phantoms, and Skyhawks, which used this new capability to conduct strikes beyond Israel's borders under the guidance of Major General Benny Peled before the arrival of the fourth generation F-16 and F-15 fighter aircraft. However, the more modern aircraft were able to expand the envelope further

Planners relied on the multi-role, two-seater F-15 Eagle aircraft configured with drop tanks to execute the mission without the need to refuel. Additionally, if armed appropriately, the selected jets would be able to carry the air-to-ground munitions as well as air-to-air weapons for self-defense, reducing the need for an armed escort mission. Thus, ten F-15 fighter aircraft were selected for the mission; eight as the primary, and two in reserve.[75]

Unlike the raid on Osirak, the IAF had mere days to prepare for the operation. Yet, the aircrew approached it with the same diligence, discipline, and attention as that pivotal strike. As Eliezer Cohen, a former Israeli fighter pilot described the mission preparations

---

[75] Cohen, 484.

in his book, *Israel's Best Defense*: "The aircrews studied the flight route, the refueling stations, and the timetables. They memorized the targets and bombing locations allocated to each aircraft. Israeli intelligence analysts added more maps, sketches, and photographs daily. The ground crews rechecked all the planes' parts and replaced anything that might cause problems."[76] Additionally, lessons learned from the fight against the PLO, Hamas, and Hezbollah added extra measures and complications for the pilots to consider.

In the fight against terrorist organizations, Israel's image and methods were under increased international and domestic scrutiny. The Israeli government placed extra emphasis on the creation of the exact damage and effect desired, as well as the limitation of collateral damage, if not complete avoidance of collateral damage. For the aircrew involved in what would be named Operation Wooden Leg, this meant using smaller munitions, and more importantly, achieving positive identification of their targets prior to initiating their bombing runs.[77] Although Israel has not provided specifics of the attack, it is suspected that they would drop 500-pound bombs instead of the readily available 2,000-pound bombs that were used in the Osirak strike.[78] The planes and crew were now ready for their mission.

The morning of October 1, 1985, arrived, and the crews were conducting last minute checks before their designated take-off times. All ten aircraft were given a last look before launching into the skies over the Mediterranean. The flight lasted a few hours before they connected with the IAF's refueling Boeing 707 near Crete and Italy. This aircraft had been converted into an aerial refueler out of necessity when the US backed out of their sale of KC-135 tanker aircraft and offered refueling Hercules C-130 aircraft instead. But the C-130 planes would not have met all the same operational requirements as a larger airplane, keeping their aerial refueling capability within operational or tactical levels and not strategic, as the IAF had envisioned it. So, the Israelis had to innovate to meet their needs.[79]

Once the ten-ship formation of fighter aircraft refueled, the primary eight pilots checked their systems and declared everything good. This was the indication to the two

---

[76] Cohen, 485.
[77] Cohen, 485.
[78] Jonathan Randal, "Israeli Air Raid Destroys Arafat's Base in Tunisia," *The Washington Post*, October 2, 1985, https://www.washingtonpost.com/archive/politics/1985/10/02/israeli-air-raid-destroys-arafats-base-in-tunisia/d98e01c3-b503-4e78-a821-02ef157bf266/?noredirect=on&utm_term=.e7bbade3690d.
[79] Cohen, *Israel's Best Defense*, 486.

aircraft in reserve to return to base. The two four-ship formations flew to their targets within the Hamas A-Shatt neighborhood. At first glance, the neighborhood appeared residential and generally inconspicuous. Had it not been for the diligent work by Israeli intelligence units, there would have been no way to distinguish a tourist's vacation home from that of the PLO leadership, Force 17's headquarters, and other terrorist group targets.

The pilots only had a few moments to visually confirm the identity of their targets against their intelligence dossiers before executing the bombing run. Among the targets selected by IAF intelligence for the strike were the Force 17 base of operations, Yasser Arafat's command center, although he was not present at the time of the strike, and a building used by the A-Tzeeka terrorist organization.[80] All eight aircraft successfully struck their assigned targets without any interference from surface-to-air or air-to-air threats. In fact, the Tunisian IADS and early warning network remained oddly quiet that morning. The strike formation returned to base without incident.

Witnesses on the ground provided inaccurate reports of the number of aircraft, the type of aircraft, and the event overall. Newspapers reported an attack by Israeli F-16 jets with other aircraft patrolling overhead. Speculation flew in diplomatic channels as to whether the US was aware of the strike when supposedly picked up by the radars of the US Sixth Fleet patrolling in the Mediterranean Sea, but deliberately did not provide early warning to Tunisian leadership. Military officials responded that the IAF's flight path and altitude would have kept it below the radars line-of-sight.[81] It was not further investigated.

Once more, the IAF was the tool by which the Israeli government could broadcast a strategic message to the world: Israel would not stand for terrorism and would hunt it down anywhere. With one strike package and action, Israel demonstrated the effectiveness and lethality of its Intelligence apparatus, planning, and long-range strike capabilities.

Conclusion

Over the course of approximately ten years and across three operations or conflicts, the Israeli Air Force showed the world that it was a force to be reckoned with both domestically and internationally. The relative peace Israel held with its neighbors opened its aperture to address other threats to its people and equities, namely that of terrorism. As

---

[80] Cohen, 487.
[81] Randal, "Israeli Air Raid Destroys Arafat's Base in Tunisia."

such, the IDF through its use of the IAF enforced national policy by striking and resisting terrorist actions that threatened the state. Israel would not be helpless in the face of terror; it would strike fear in the heart of terror with an airpower delivered solution.

Chapter 5

Conclusion

Even during stormy times such as the one being faced by the countries surrounding us and the voice of their people is ever growing, we see the mission that we must fulfill- our duty to stand firm and to be alert, watching over Israel, and be ready to face any challenge.

Lt. Gen. Benny Gantz
IDF Chief of Staff, 1997

Modern-day perceptions of premier air forces spark imagery in the minds of airpower enthusiasts globally of the US, Chinese, Russian, other large states' air forces, and the Israeli Air Force (IAF). Israel's air power evolution is unique from the others in the compressed timeline and political context under which it evolved. Much of the literature surrounding the IAF has been mostly descriptive rather than analytical. Any analysis has had an operational or tactical focus, exploring how the IAF attained air superiority or conducted precision strikes. To begin to fill the gap in the scholarship of the IAF as a tool of national power, this thesis traced the IAF's evolution from its inception in 1947 to its first few manifestations of a tool of national power. With this analysis, this thesis sought to answer these central questions: what factors have influenced the evolution of the Israeli Air Force from 1947 until it became a national level tool?

The Israeli Air Force was selected for this purpose as it presents a prime case study in air force evolution. The compressed and eventful timeline highlights distinct evolutionary steps, inflection points, and changes that progressed the IAF from a tactical to a strategic tool of national power. Following its significant campaigns, this thesis identified many factors that contributed to the efficacy of the IAF at its intended level of utilization and the catalysts to change that led to the two inflection points that characterize the next step the IAF's evolution.

The Chronology

The state of Israel was established in a politically volatile period that heavily influenced the birth and development of the Israel Defense Forces (IDF) and the IAF. As Israel worked towards protecting its newfound sovereignty, the IDF and IAF had one primary goal: to defend the nation, ensuring its survival. This goal would prove difficult for the small state lacking geographic, economic, and military strategic depth.

The War of Independence in 1948 was the IAF's debut after it transitioned from the *Sherut Avir,* Air Service, to the formal air force. The IAF personnel ranged from recruit to experienced combat aviator. The airplanes and equipment were mostly civilian in origin (See Table 1 in Chapter Two). The IAF training, tactics, techniques, plans, procedures, and processes were practically non-existent at the onset and slowly came to be standardized through the days of combat and operations. Civilian aircraft were reconfigured to meet military needs until military aircraft specifically designed for military missions arrived. Even so, the IDF assigned the IAF to support the ground forces commanders, subordinating air operations to ground priorities. The IAF was thus utilized initially as aerial reconnaissance and improvised bombing, expanding to include troop transport, interdiction, air-to-air combat, and bombing missions with the new military aircraft. The IAF conducted its first offensive air strike as part of Operation Yoav in October 1948. The IAF's role in Operation Yoav was to reduce the threat of adversary forces in the Negev Desert to enable IDF control of the area which subsequently resulted in an expansion of the country's borders once the ceasefire was emplaced in the spring of 1949.

During the ceasefire and relative peace that followed, the IDF and IAF took a moment for reflection, self-evaluation, and future force planning. The IAF faced challenges in securing support and the budget to posture the force for what its leaders perceived as the future air war. It was not until Major General Dan Tolkovski accepted command of the IAF that progress was made in this regard. Tolkovski kickstarted integrated planning for personnel, equipment, aircraft, resources, and missions that led to a comprehensive reform of the IAF. The new IAF airman and his aircraft would compensate for its small numbers in higher overall quality, better plans and tactics, and an efficiency that would remain unrivaled in the region.

The first test for the new IAF came in the form of the Suez Canal Crisis in 1956. For this event, Israel allied with England and France to regain control over Suez Canal operations from Egypt who had declared it an Egyptian national asset. As the nations worked together on a plan, the IDF assigned the IAF the opening move in the coalition action. Thus, Operation Kadesh began with a deception campaign and surprise air strike against the Egyptian Air Force. Operation Kadesh was significant in several ways; it was the first time that the IAF could test the results of its reform under Tolkovski in training, tactics, strategy, and airplane acquisition. The highly qualified pilots executed the preemptive strategy against the Egyptian airfields so well that about 80% of the Egyptian air force inventory was destroyed while on the ground. Also, it represented an initial IDF understanding of the necessity of air superiority before the subordination of airpower to ground objectives, and translated into a new military doctrine shift for the IDF. No longer was the doctrine surrounding solely ground forces, but a new combined airpower and armor doctrine took hold. The success and lessons of the Suez Canal Crisis further prepared the IDF for the Six Day War a decade later.

The preparation for the 1967 Six-Day War and planning for Operation *Moked,* began over ten years earlier under the guidance of Major General Tolkovski's doctrinal and planning reforms. The air strikes in the Suez Canal Crisis cemented the necessity for achieving air superiority via an initial offensive strike Also, as the IDF planners crafted branch plans for war with a variety of hostile neighbors, Tolkovski's priority for an offensive air strike against the enemy air force became an Operation *Moked* objective. The IAF execution of Operation *Moked* was nearly flawless. Once more, beginning with a denial and deception campaign, the IAF operation caught the Egyptian and Syrian air forces unaware. Additionally, the IAF's finely tuned sortie execution and aircraft regeneration rate were so fast that the enemy air forces were unable to react quickly enough to limit damage to their forces. Additionally, at the end of the first day's operations, the IAF had seriously maimed the Arab air forces and reinforced the power and utility of the IAF to create strategic effects in the immediate battlespace.

After Operation *Moked* and the Six-Day War, the Israelis had more geographic strategic depth, but the land acquired also stretched thin its few forces. Additionally, the IAF had lost up to 20% of its aircraft of various types, increasing the burden on those that remained. Lastly, although Israel viewed the war as over, the Egyptian perspective of the results of the Six-Day War, al-Naksa, or the setback, colored its actions for the next six years as it pursued actions against Israel until the Yom Kippur War.

This period became known as the War of Attrition as the Egyptian military staged harassing strikes and operations against southern Israel. It was able to do so due to the infusion of technology and equipment that the Soviet Union provided at President Nasser's request. The Soviet support had a paradoxical effect to the military balance of power in that region as it prompted the US to support Israel in a similar vein as the two great powers used the Middle East as a proxy setting. Thus, the IDF continued its equipment modernization and IAF expansion with American technology. Additionally, the success of the Six Day War and a lack of operation self-reflection during the War of Attrition caused the IDF's military strategy and doctrine to stagnate with few updates derived from the changing operational environment.

In response to the Egyptian attacks in the Sinai during the War of Attrition, the IAF was summoned as flying artillery to destroy the Egyptian artillery and air threats that threatened the ground forces in the peninsula. Again, the IAF was subordinated to the ground forces commander and ground requirements. Only in Operation Priha was the IAF used in an offensive strike capacity against the Egyptian IADS, ground units, and other targets. This operation prompted the Soviet Union to provide the Egyptians with an advanced Soviet Integrated Air Defense Systems (IADS), and expertise updating Arab military capabilities, reach, and tactics. Despite operations and losses within the engagement zones of the updated IADS, the IAF only responded to some of the advancements in the Arab capabilities. This lack of preparation for the next war would be detrimental to the IAF performance in the Yom Kippur War.

Several significant issues compounded to make the Yom Kippur War a negative experience for Israel. First, the country's civilian leadership elected to forego a preemptive strike to preserve international support and provide the justification of self-defense. Second, the IAF had slackened somewhat in its rigor of training and preparation for war, due to a hubris and belief that it was still the premier air force in the region. Third, the Israelis failed to account fully for the Egyptian IADS buildup and its implications for Israeli operations. Fourth, the Arab militaries entered the conflict with limited objectives, refusing to play to the advantages of the IDF and luring the IDF and IAF into increasingly disadvantageous battles.

The Arab militaries were first to strike, placing the IDF in a defensive and reactionary role from the start. This narrowed Israel's scope of operation and effect to that of defeating of enemy attacks rather than creating a strategic effect in the adversary system. Once the IAF regrouped after the initial attacks, it launched Operational Plans Tagar 4 and 5, attempting to gain a measure of air freedom of maneuver. These operations did not have the desired effect on the battlespace. Next, the IAF executed Operation Dugman, initially planning for a strike against the Egyptian IADS, but ultimately targeting the Syrian IADS with limited success.

Despite many mistakes and failures during the Yom Kippur War, the air raid on the Syrian General Command stands out as a success. In retaliation for the Syrian missile barrage of northern Israel, and in hopes of deterring Jordan from entering the fray, Israel launched a strike deep into the heart of the Syrian capital. The desired effects of the strike were strategic, intending to create strategic, moral, and psychological impacts on the Syrian citizens and leaders to pause if not end hostilities entirely. Ultimately, the Yom Kippur War was an exercise in survival and mitigation of losses. The nearly three-week war took a toll on the IDF and IAF specifically, prompting Major General Benny Peled, the IAF Chief, to conduct a fresh round of reforms within the IAF.

Two major findings from post-war investigations prompted the IAF reforms; the IAF had not acted as a preemptive and preventative force before the war, and it had not won the air war. The IAF transformed its war plans, changing the underlying assumptions, timing, and preparedness functions. Organizationally, it established an autonomous IAF branch for intelligence needs and incorporated the anti-aircraft artillery units from the ground forces, consolidating that chain of command. Money and time were invested into the growing domestic technology and military industry to pursue modernized equipment that would offset the advantages of the Soviet-provided equipment to the Arabs. The IAF invested in unmanned aerial vehicles, helicopters, refueling capabilities, joint exercises, and ground and airborne command and control capabilities.

Concurrent with the internal changes of the IDF and IAF, the regional context in which Israel existed changed. The Yom Kippur War would be the last large force-on-force war in which it would participate till current day. After 1973, the IAF's aperture for operations would widen as the nation faced different types of threats across the region and globe.

The first such operation was Operation Thunderbolt, in which pro-Palestinian terrorists hijacked an Air France flight and diverted it to Uganda, keeping it hostage until their demands would be met. While Israel was confronted with the choice of negotiating with the terrorists, the IAF was presented with a mobility challenge. The IAF needed to deliver a sizeable assault force, command and control capability, and medical team thousands of miles away to the Entebbe airport in Uganda, in a possibly contested environment without aerial refueling. Although Operation Thunderbolt experienced setbacks, the IAF's execution of the operation was as successful as possible. Operation Thunderbolt represents a strategic application of airpower, not "independent", but as a critical and necessary component of a joint operation conducted thousands of miles from Israel itself – and with minimal outside assistance.

The terrorist threat was not limited to hijacking and the odd attack. A population of Arabs disaffected by their countries' peace treaties and ceasefires with Israel took the situation in their own hands. Groups of terrorists sought sanctuary in Lebanon, establishing a base of operations from which to attack the IDF and Israel writ large. After the Israeli threshold of attacks on IDF soldiers was crossed, the Israeli leadership elected to leverage the IAF's precision strike capabilities in both retaliation for and preemption of further terrorist attacks. The goals of these strikes were to influence the behavior of Palestinian and Lebanese terrorist organizations, rather than destroy specific functions of the groups themselves. The strikes themselves were a success tactically, precisely affecting the targets that Israeli intelligence recommended while limiting collateral damage to the civilian surroundings. However, the use of airpower to change behavior in this situation was less effective, and the attacks against northern Israel continued.

A second operation that tested the limits of the IAF's capabilities was Operation Babylon, the 1981 attack on the Osirak nuclear reactor in Baghdad. For years, Saddam Hussein led Iraq in pursuit of nuclear power and weapons. In the Israeli perspective, the nuclear program coupled with Hussein's rhetoric represented an existential threat to the state. To set back the Iraqi nuclear program, Israel launched a complex air operation. Israeli intelligence built the dossier on the nuclear program for over five years, exploiting information from many forms of sources and through many methods. The intelligence remained ready awaiting authorization for an operation.

When the Israeli leadership believed that time was running out to strike the reactor before it achieved operational status, it authorized the planning and strike. The IAF planners designed the detailed operation down to the second, and the aircrew who were to execute it spent nearly a year in training for the strike. The strike itself, conducted on

June 7, 1981, was near flawless in execution. The IAF utilized its newest aircraft, the F-16 and F-15 fighters, configured with drop tanks and specific munitions to conduct the strike and provide fighter escort respectively. The mixed formation flew the 2,500-kilometer round trip without any problems. The strike itself was executed as planned, down to the second, and in three minutes of the bombing, both the Iraqi nuclear reactors were destroyed. This operation was the first successful preemptive strike against a nuclear installation in history and expanded the understanding of strategic deterrence to that which could be accomplished by conventional means. Additionally, Operation Babylon reinforced the message that the IAF's reach went beyond its immediate vicinity.

The final operation that demonstrated Israel's ability to project its national will abroad via its air force was the 1985 strike on the Palestinian Liberation Organization (PLO) headquarters in Tunisia titled Operation Wooden Leg. PLO leaders had fled from Beirut to Tunisia as a result of IDF operations against them in Lebanon. As Israeli intelligence continued to track them in Tunisia, it was suspected that the Force 17 unit of the PLO murdered three Israelis in the port of Larnaca, Cyprus. As a result of this strike, the Israeli leadership decided on a retaliatory action in Tunis, Tunisia to demonstrate the vulnerability of terrorists who threaten the people of Israel.

The strike in Tunis became the longest range strike the IAF would conduct to date, ranging 2,400 kilometers one way. Unlike Operation Thunderbolt, in which the IAF had a year to prepare, the aircrew had only a fraction of the time to ready themselves for this long-range surgical strike. Leveraging its newfound aerial refueling capability, the formation of F-15 Eagles soared through the Mediterranean without the need to land and soon arrived at the target area undetected.

Within minutes of crossing into Tunisian airspace, the F-15s were over their respective targets. The pilots had mere seconds to attain positive visual identification of the target based upon intelligence and to release their munitions. All eight aircraft successfully struck their targets while limiting collateral damage to the surrounding buildings. Before the Tunisian IADS or leadership could react, the strike was complete, and the Israeli fighter jets returned to Israel triumphant and untouched. News reporting from Tunisia as well as US intelligence analysts indicated that the skill and precision with which the Israelis had planned and struck terrorist targets in Tunisia, had earned it a place amongst the premier air forces in the world.

Inflection Points

The historical narrative highlights two inflection points that changed the trajectory of the IAF. The first was the tenure and guidance of Major General Dan Tolkovski from 1953-1958 and the second was the momentous pivot of the IAF under the leadership of Major General Benny Peled following the Yom Kippur War. These inflection points divide the history of the IAF into three distinct periods: the 1948 war of independence to the 1967 Six Day War, the Egyptian al-Naksa of 1967 to the 1973 Yom Kippur War, and the post-Yom Kippur War to the 1985 strike on the Palestinian Liberation Organization headquarters in Tunisia.

Both generals assessed the contemporary state of the IAF as insufficient for the future needs of the nation's defense. This assessment derived from their views on the utilization of air power in the War of Independence for Tolkovski and Yom Kippur War for Peled. The failures and shortcomings of IAF utilization and capability in those wars sparked ideas in the minds of both generals that would challenge the respective anachronistic paradigms of the force. Thus, both generals leveraged lessons learned from their respective conflicts to build new paradigms of the IAF's capability, capacity, size, and utilization.

Prior to 1953, Israeli leaders had limited vision of the utility and purpose of their air force. In their minds, the sole purpose of the air force was to further ground objectives and victories. Limited air superiority was a necessary air objective to enable air support to the ground scheme of maneuver. Tolkovski was the first IAF general to challenge this paradigm successfully. He asserted that air superiority would be the lynchpin to any future IDF operation.

Additionally, the disproportionate inventories of a small state like Israel to that of its larger enemies would entail thorough future operational planning and the need for a preemptive strike. The preemptive strike would ideally destroy the opposing air force while it was still on the ground, thus increasing the survivability of the IAF strike force and future air operations in that conflict as a lesser enemy force would remain. Tolkovski knew this would require efficiency and precision that the IAF had yet to achieve, so he singlehandedly raised the operating standards of the IAF personnel as well as ameliorated some of that transition. To reduce the difficulty of attaining such high standards, Tolkovski pursued an equipment modernization and standardization effort. His idea was that by limiting the number of types of airframes and support equipment necessary, he could reduce the initial training time of support personnel and also speed up the timeline to the technical proficiency and then expertise in ground support roles. This would help reduce the flight turn-around times and allow the IAF to maximize its strategic surprise in Tolkovski's proposed preemptive attacks.

Major General Benny Peled's vision of the new IAF grew out of the failures of the Yom Kippur War. After the war, Peled ordered investigations and evaluations to identify the flaws and gaps of its performance. The investigations found that the IAF had failed at in two core areas: it had not acted as a preemptive and preventative force before the war, and it had not won the air war. This prompted Peled to conduct service-wide reforms.

Organizationally, the reforms included growing the intelligence branch of the IAF, to ensure that timely intelligence that specialized in supporting air operations was delivered to the IAF decisionmakers without delay. Secondary effects were that collected data and images that could feed into subsequent air missions were exploited into intelligence and provided to the tactical units without always having to trickle down from above. Additionally, the anti-aircraft artillery units were removed from the IDF ground units and subordinated to the IAF. This also meant they now came under the efficiency and quality demands of the Major General Tolkosvki's legacy, in that they would have to train and respond to a higher standard.

The reforms affected operational and strategic planning assumptions, changing plans on the shelf. Tactically, pilots integrated modern technology into their operating procedures, increasing reliance on electronic warfare and beyond-visual-range air-to-air missiles. The reforms also fed into Israel's technocratic technological industry prompting research into more effective missiles for IADS targets, electronic warfare, computers for flight control in complex electronic environments, long-range missiles, and more. The IAF now operated within a new paradigm; that with available resources, it was critical to select the weapons and aircraft that could create the most substantial and most desired effect with the least amount of dedicated resources.

Thus, the IAF pursued purchases of airframes and equipment that would satisfy the most mission requirements in the smartest and most survivable ways possible. As such, the IAF increased investment in unmanned aerial vehicles (UAV). Although initially used as decoys for IADS, they also doubled as intelligence, surveillance, and reconnaissance platforms. For similar quality photography and data, they were employed for a fraction of the cost, both financial and human, with minimum risk to the aircrew. Transport aircraft with longer ranges were acquired. Additionally, the IAF invested in helicopters with transport and attack capabilities.

The last financial investment was in the realm of command and control. In an effort to streamline command and control of air operations, the IAF leaders needed a clear picture of both air and ground operations to guide their relatively few assets effectively. The change to command and control would be reliant on intelligence, surveillance, and reconnaissance assets that could provide an up-to-date operating picture for the commander of the air war. This is modernly referred to as a common operating picture. To enable this, the IAF developed a communications infrastructure that could support the common operating picture and the IAF commanders' near-real-time direction of the air scheme of maneuver.

Doctrinally the IAF expanded its focus as well. Peled understood the need for interoperability with the IDF ground forces and pushed the IAF into joint exercises. It even assigned air liaison officers to ground units to enhance communications. Through increased interaction and interoperability, Peled was able to advocate for battlefield interdiction and ground attack before the troops came into contact, limiting the risk of fratricide and decreasing limitations on pilots conducting those strikes.

The last major reform entailed the IAF's training for strike missions. Peled was also able to advocate for the doctrinal importance of deep and strategic attack. Thus, the IAF trained with a high priority on attack and long-range strike missions. These training missions were further enabled by the newly acquired airborne command and control aircraft. With these changes, Peled was able to revitalize the IAF, bringing it back to the forefront of capability and modernity.

Evolutionary Factors

Although the inflection points are specific instances that changed the direction of the IAF's evolution, they are not the sole driving forces behind it. This thesis highlighted several factors that influenced or demonstrated the evolutionary steps of the IAF on its journey from tactical to a strategic tool of national power. These factors all play different roles in influencing air force evolution and can contextually have more or less impact when applied to different case studies.

Existential threat and geography. The near-constant existential threat, time, necessity, and lack of strategic depth had significant influence over the evolution of the IAF. When Israel's immediate geographic neighbors posed the existential threat to the state, then the urgency of action was high. Paradoxically, the proximity lowered the threshold to create a strategic effect in those adversary countries. The short distances meant that specialized aircraft and equipment would not be needed to reach those destinations. When the immediate vicinity stabilized, and Israel was able to look further out into the region and world for threats, then the need for specialized capabilities increased in order to create those strategic effects at a time and place of Israel's choosing.

Intent. Air power is merely a tool, a piece of technology, that acts in the way for which its owners plan. The level at which those actions create effects has more to do with the intent of the decision makers and planners. Strategic effects depend on the intent of the outcome that is generated and less on the action or tool itself. A bomber can drop a munition on a headquarters building to stymie the command and control of an adversary operation, and it can use that same bomb against that same headquarters building to send a strategic message of vulnerability to the adversary leaders. Again, it is the intent with which the decision makers deploy those capabilities that determine the level at which the air force operates.

Air-mindedness of leaders. An influencing factor on the establishment of the intent with which an action has been decided is the air-mindedness of those same leaders. As Billy Mitchell once pointed out in his book *Winged Defense,* in order to maximize on the medium of air, it has to be understood. "People who are unused to or unfamiliar with air work are incapable of visioning what air power should be, of training the men necessary for work in the air, or of devising the equipment that they should have."

[1] In contrast to the situation in which Mitchell found himself advocating for an air force and airpower in a period of peace that would last twenty years, the IAF generals started in a more air-minded environment. The civilian and IDF leaders established the air force as a separate branch from the beginning, not enduring the tumultuous tug-of-war over airpower independence.

Additionally, the feedback loop built into war and combat operations was much tighter for the IDF leaders. Although they initially subordinated airpower to the ground commander, it did not take long before the IAF's missions would be controlled by IAF leaders, prioritizing enabling effects of airpower over the battlespace before supporting ground troops. Lastly, the Israeli mandatory service requirements resulted in more civilian leaders with military and combat experience, that had seen the effects of airpower first-hand and could better understand the power that the IAF could bring to the fight.

Technology and acquisition. The fundamental understanding of the potential of airpower led to a vision of what was needed to maximize that potential. As mentioned, Israel is a small state of little strategic depth geographically, demographically, and economically. Thus, the IAF had to be strategic in its future inventory and capability plans. Under Tolkovski, the IAF pursued a realistic and balanced acquisition plan. The purpose was to reduce the variety of equipment while satisfying the many mission requirements the IAF would have leveraged upon it. Later, under Peled, the IAF would modernize its fleet through purchase or domestic customization of the purchased aircraft. He would expand the capabilities of the IAF to meet the new intent of inter-regional and global effect. In addition to the fighter, bomber, and transport aircraft, the IAF invested in helicopters, electronic countermeasures, UAVs, and other technology.

A bonus factor that occurred as a result of the increasing need for technology and the perceived potential for international support and arms deals, the Israeli government bolstered the Israeli military and technological industries. Israeli accepted a technocratic state mindset to drive domestic research and development in support of the military, and specifically, aircraft, weapons, and advanced capabilities. In this way, it could tailor its research and development, cutting down on time from conception to implementation of

---

[1] William Mitchell, *Winged Defense: The Development and Possibilities of Modern Air Power--Economic and Military* (Tuscaloosa, AL: University of Alabama Press, 2009), 160.

operational capabilities as well as reliance on foreign suppliers. The technology acquisition and development were driven by, and an influencing factor for, the evolution of IAF doctrine and its updated prioritized mission sets of deep strike, interdiction, and CAS.

Divestment of missions and the multirole capability. The integration of helicopters and unmanned aerial vehicles into the IAF inventory enabled IAF leaders and planners to divest the fighters and bombers of mission sets that were limiting the allocation of airpower to more strategic objectives. This enabled the concentrated use of the manned fighters and bombers on high priority and effect missions. This drove doctrinal changes that encompassed the purpose, utilization, and preparation for the use of airpower in combat and to strategic effect.

Quality and standards. As Tolkovski inherently understood, it is more than the technology that makes a capable air force. His emphasis on quality personnel, training, and higher standards remains the status-quo today. Today, modern IAF aircrew applicants, for example, undergo one of the longest and most challenging officer accession and aircrew training programs. The three-year program occurs in five phases, covering the basics of flight, officership, strategy, science, mathematics, and their specific aircrew positions.[2] As such, the acceptance criteria to the IAF for aircrew positions is high, but even so, the washout rate for the program is also high. The IAF ensures that the quality of personnel that is pushed onto the field is as close to perfect as possible because they cannot afford to have anything less than that. This high standard and quality of the IAF Airman continue to earn it a place amongst the top air forces in the world.

Recommendations for further study

Israel presents an interesting case study in the evolution of air forces in that the transformation of the state's flying capability transformed rapidly over approximately thirty-four years. This thesis has identified the inflection points of this transformation within the IAF's evolution and characteristics that contributed to the evolutionary steps. With this information, I submit that a theory of how small state air forces develop can be inductively hypothesized. Further study could validate the theory against other small state's air forces and establish its explanatory, categorization, and anticipatory value.

---

[2] "How IAF Pilots Take Off," Israeli Defense Force, 2018, https://www.idf.il/en/minisites/israeli-air-force/how-iaf-pilots-take-off/.

Although this thesis has identified inflection points and evolutionary factors that contributed to the IAF's evolution from tactical to strategic, it is essential to note the importance of context when applying the theory to different cases. The context will be how a country's leaders will understand the purpose and utility of the air force. In Israel's case, being a small country surrounded on three sides by enemies with capable air forces meant that the IAF would have to meet and exceed those challenges. Thus, an existential threat and the proximity of said threat will play a large part in determining the mission requirements for the nation's air force and the role it will play in the nation's military.

Additionally, the air-mindedness or state leaders' vision for the use of the air force will lead it down various paths. That vision will influence investment, growth, and the priority the air force receives in contrast to the rest of the military. It is the intent of those leaders coupled with the capabilities present that will ultimately mark the transformation of the air force to a national and strategic tool of power.

BIBLIOGRAPHY

Arkin, William M. "Driving Victory. Airpower in the 2006 Israel-Hezbollah War." Air University, 2007.

Bar-Joseph, Uri, Amos Perlmutter, and Michael I. Handel. *Two Minutes Over Baghdad*. Second. New York: Routledge Taylor & Francis Group, 2003.

Bean, James W, and Craig S Girard. "Anwar Al-Sadat's Grand Strategy in the Yom Kippur War." *National War College*, 2001, 1–20. http://www.dtic.mil/dtic/tr/fulltext/u2/a442407.pdf.

Bluestone, B L, and J P Peak. "Air Superiority and Airfield Attack - Lessons From History." McLean, VA, 1984.

Bowen, Jeremy. *Six Days*. New York: St. Martin's Press, 2005.

Braut-Hegghammer, Malfrid. *Unclear Physics; Why Iraq and Libya Failed to Build Nuclear Weapons*. Ithaca, NY: Cornell University Press, 2016.

Bregman, Ahron. *Israel's Wars. Israel's Wars*, 2016. https://doi.org/10.4324/9781315646893.

Brun, Itai. "The Second Lebanon War, 2006." In *A History of Air Warfare*, 2010.

Carter, Jr., John R. "Airpower and the Cult of the Offensive." Air University, 1998.

Cohen, Eliezer. *Israel's Best Defense*. New York: Orion Books, 1993.

Corum, James S., and Wray R. Johnson. *Airpower in Small Wars: Fighting Insurgents and Terrorists*. Lawrence, KS: University Press of Kansas, 2003.

David, Saul. *Operation Thunderbolt: Flight 139 and the Raid on Entebbe Airport, the Most Audacious Hostage Rescue Mission in History*. New York: Little, Brown, 2015.

Doyle, Joseph S. "The Yom Kippur War and the Shaping of the United States Air Force." School of Advanced Air and Space Studies Air University, 2016.

Dunstan, Simon. *The Six Day War 1967: Jordan and Syria*. Long Island City: Osprey Publishing, 2009.

———. *The Six Day War 1967: Sinai*. Long Island City: Osprey Publishing, 2009.

Farley, Robert. "The Inside Story of How Israel's Air Force Dominates the Sky (And Crushes Its Enemies)." *The National Interest*, October 2018.

"Federal Police - GSG 9 Der Bundespolizei." Accessed April 25, 2019. https://web.archive.org/web/20160522195149/http://www.bundespolizei.de/Web/DE/05Die-Bundespolizei/04Einsatzkraefte/03GSG9/GSG9_node.html.

Frank J. Prial. "Israeli Planes Attack P.L.O. in Tunis, Killing At Least 30; Raid 'Legitimate.'" *New York Times*, October 2, 1985. https://www.nytimes.com/1985/10/02/world/israeli-planes-attack-plo-in-tunis-killing-at-least-30-raid-legitimate-us-says.html.

Givens, Robert P. "Turning the Vertical Flank: Airpower as a Maneuver Force in the Theater Campaign." School of Advanced Air and Space Studies Air University, 2001.

Gordon, Shmuel L. "Air Superiority in the Arab Israeli Wars, 1967-1982." In *A History of Air Warfare*, 127–56. Dulles, VA: Potomac Books, 2010.

Griess, Thomas E, Roy K Flint, and United States Military Academy. Dept. of History. "Atlas of the Arab-Israeli Wars, the Chinese Civil War, and the Korean War." *The West Point Military History Series*, 1986. https://doi.org/10.1109/TRO.2007.904911.

Hadar, Moshe; Ofer, Yehuda;, ed. *Heyl Haavir Israel Air Force*. Tel Aviv, Israel: Pell Printing Words, Ltd, 1971.

Hicks, J. Marcus. "Fire in the City Airpower in Urban, Smaller-Scale Contingencies." School of Advanced Airpower Studies Air University, 1999.

Higham, Robin D. S, and Stephen John Harris. *Why Air Force Fail: The Anatomy of Defeat*. Lexington, KY: University Press of Kentucky, 2006.

"How IAF Pilots Take Off." Israeli Defense Force, 2018. https://www.idf.il/en/minisites/israeli-air-force/how-iaf-pilots-take-off/.

Jordan, Jarret D. "The Trinity in Balance: Israel's Strategy for Victory in the Six Day War." National Defense University National War College Washington, 2000.

Kis, Ervin J. "Techniques of Gaining Israeli Air Superiority in the 1973 War, Better Known as ' The Yom Kippur War '" 7, no. 3 (2008): 407–23.

Lailari, Guermantes E, Advisor Major, Gregory Stanley, Maxwell Air, and Force Base. "Israel's National Missile Defense Strategy (Abridged Version)," no. April (2001).

Lambeth, Benjamin S, Rand Corporation., and Project Air Force (U.S.). *Air Operations in Israel's War against Hezbollah : Learning from Lebanon and Getting It Right in Gaza*, 2011. http://www.rand.org/content/dam/rand/pubs/monographs/2011/RAND_MG835.pdf.

Lapidot, Aharon, ed. *Open Skies שמיים נקיים: The Israeli Air Force: 40 Years*. Tel Aviv, Israel: Israeli Ministry of Defense and Peli Press, 1998.

Levine, Todd J. "Into the Lion's Den: A Matter of Israeli Survival," 2004.

Levitan, Eliyah. "The Israeli Air Force: Operation Priha," 2016. http://www.iaf.org.il/4443-46087-en/IAF.aspx.

Mitchell, William. *Winged Defense: The Development and Possibilities of Modern Air Power-- Economic and Military*. Tuscaloosa, AL: University of Alabama Press, 2009.

"Operation Wooden Leg." Accessed November 4, 2019. https://www.idf.il/en/minisites/wars-and-operations/operation-wooden-leg-1985/.

Peres, Shimon. *No Room for Small Dreams: Courage, Imagination and the Making of Modern Israel*. UK: Hachette, 2017.

Phillips, Mark D. "Deception , Surprise and Attack : Operational Art for Air Superiority." Naval War College, 2006.

Randal, Jonathan. "Israel's Air Raid Destroys Arafat's Base in Tunisia." *CIA Archives: The Washington Post*, October 2, 1985. https://www.cia.gov/library/readingroom/docs/CIA-RDP90-00965R000605360009-6.pdf.

———. "Israeli Air Raid Destroys Arafat's Base in Tunisia." *The Washington Post*, October 2,

1985. https://www.washingtonpost.com/archive/politics/1985/10/02/israeli-air-raid-destroys-arafats-base-in-tunisia/d98e01c3-b503-4e78-a821-02ef157bf266/?noredirect=on&utm_term=.e7bbade3690d.

Rodman, David. *Sword and Shield of Zion : The Israel Air Force in the Arab-Israeli Conflict, 1948-2012*. Portland, OR: Sussex Academic Press, 2013.

———. "The Six Day War, 1967: Sinai/The Six Day War, 1967: Jordan and Syria." *Israel Affairs*, 2011.

Rubenstein, Murray, and Richard Goldman. *Shield of David*. Englewood-Cliffs, New Jersey: Prentice-Hall, 1978.

Schiff, Zeev, and Ehud Ya'ari. *Israel's Lebanon War*. New York: Simon and Schuster, 1984.

Show Jr, Kenneth C. "Falcons Against Jihad." Air University, 1995.

Springer, Rita A. "Operation Moked and the Principles of War." Naval War College, 1997.

"The Israeli Air Force, Mission Statement." Accessed December 4, 2018. http://www.iaf.org.il/34-en/IAF.aspx.

"The Israeli Air Force: 1970s Events Log." Accessed April 3, 2019. http://www.iaf.org.il/837-7128-en/IAF.aspx.

"The Israeli Air Force: The Next Generation of the Intelligence Division Learns From the Past," 2014. http://www.iaf.org.il/4404-41452-EN/IAF.aspx.

"World Atlas, Geography of Israel." Accessed December 4, 2018. https://www.worldatlas.com/webimage/countrys/asia/israel/illand.htm.